TABLE OF CONTENTS

ILLUSTRATIONS

TABLES

CHAPTER 1

INTRODUCTION

Introduction and Background

A military purist may say that a nation's military exists for the sole purpose of winning that nation's wars. While most would agree that winning a nation's wars is indeed a prime purpose for a military, that purpose is not the sole reason for a military's existence. Admiral Gary Roughead, the U.S. Chief of Naval Operations, stated in the Naval Operations Concept 2010 document, coordinated with the Navy, Marine Corps, and Coast Guard, that —We do more than just respond; we prevent."[1]

The document, known as the NOC, continues, —In our Maritime Strategy we state that it is just as important to prevent wars as it is to win wars. That is done through our worldwide presence, our well-trained Sailors, and our very capable ships, airplanes, and submarines."[2] The NOC may have used the word prevent here inaccurately (more on that later in chapter 2), but the point is still taken that merely winning current wars is no longer the military's sole purpose.

Not to be outdone, the U.S. Army's Operating Concept (AOC), 2016-2028 describes how future Army forces conduct operations as part of the joint force to *deter conflict*, prevail in war, and succeed in a wide range of contingencies in the future operational environment (emphasis is author's).[3]

So, if it really is as important to prevent (or deter or preempt) wars from happening in the first place as it is to win them once started, then it would be reasonable to assume that allocation of the military's overall resources, to include manpower, training, and equipment would be dedicated in sufficient levels to support those deterrence efforts. What those "sufficient levels" equate to remains outside the scope of this thesis, but a quick statistic about Class 11-01 at the Army's Command and General Staff School (ILE) course suggests a few changes that could make a difference. Current ILE curriculum offers two Security Cooperation courses, but remains outside the core as elective courses only. One classified course is for U.S. students only, and the other unclassified course is formatted for all interested students. Of the 1,056 total students, only 48 elected to take either course format. This breaks down to approximately 4.5 percent of the student body, with further analysis revealing that a mere 3.9 percent of U.S. students and 17.4 percent of international students chose to learn more about security cooperation.

Containment consists of a specific collection of tools and coordinated policies, including the threat of military force, designed to keep its target in check. Its success relies on deterrent effect. While many military leaders have minimal training on overall deterrence, most have even less on specific containment strategies.

Containment, as a policy and strategy, originally developed as a long-term U.S. response to Stalin's leadership of the Soviet Union after World War II (WWII) ended. That version of containment used various deterrence principles and methods in a coordinated effort designed to prevent expansion of Soviet influence. The policy's main proponent and creator, George Kennan, believed that patient, consistent, and enduring application of containment would eventually convince the Kremlin, though probably not Stalin himself, that drastic reform would be required to compete with the capitalist systems of the free world.[4] This thesis specifically addresses how containment policies evolved from the Cold War era to the present day, and then evaluates modern individual cases against the backdrop of Cold War containment principles to assess potential effectiveness.

Significance

A baseline level of knowledge about containment and how it fit into the history of United States' (U.S.) National Security Strategy is useful to the military professional. While the use of military power was a single element of containment policy, it was a crucial one, especially throughout the Cold War. Politicians and policy makers relied on their understanding of history, personal philosophies, world-views, and civilian and military advisors to shape and implement the course of national policies.

If a post-Cold War politician contemplates a military iteration of containment for application against an entity today, it is incumbent upon the military professional to offer his or her informed assessment and advice up through the chain of command for consideration by the policy maker.

This thesis reviews the major theories of war through the lens of the Cold War and its various containment policies configurations, and discerns whether elements of containment can be effective against non-superpower targets. Armed with this knowledge, military leaders will be better equipped to provide well-considered advice to their leadership.

Problem Statement

Current debate exists regarding containment's relevance in current U.S. foreign policy. Some argue containment policy died along with the Soviet Union, and is no longer a viable course of action, while others argue the opposite, and is still helpful in generating foreign policy even today. A critical analysis of selected post-Cold War case studies, while not definitively settling the debate, will certainly provide useful information to political policy makers and supporting military advisors.

As previously mentioned, containment policy during the Cold War was a critical component of overall U.S. foreign policy and national security policy. Designed originally as a strategy to deal with the Kremlin's perceived proclivities to expand its global sphere of influence and dominance, U.S. containment policy ultimately proved superior to Russian-style communism. Containment's success spawned enduring questions pertaining to its applicability to situations other than against a super power peer. Do legacy elements of containment still work when applied to a lesser adversary? Many foreign policy practitioners cling to the ideals espoused by Cold War containment practices. This therefore biases them toward the belief that similar principles will be just as effective if implemented toward modern threats, despite the facts that Cold War containment applied solely against a peer super power, and did not have attached timelines to accomplish its ultimate goal. Are there any universally applicable generalized containment components, or was it strictly limited to the Soviet Union Cold War application? In other words, does containment have a legitimate role in U.S. foreign policy today when the U.S. is the only remaining super power?

For containment to be effective, Diplomatic, Information, Military and Economic (DIME) policies must combine in a fashion that achieves the goal of preventing the containee from expanding its influence beyond a set boundary previously determined by the containing country. Credible and capable forces must exist in order to send an unambiguous message to the containment target that policy enforcement and accompanying unacceptable levels of inflicted pain is a real possibility if containment efforts are unpersuasive. That credible force is traditionally associated with the military, and manifested via tools such as multinational Theater Security Cooperation (TSC) programs and exercises, unilateral regional exercises, and Flexible Deterrent Options (FDOs). Despite these existing tools, many military professionals have limited training and education about their strategic, operational and tactical roles and responsibilities in planning and executing broader U.S. policy, especially as it relates to nesting within the National Security Strategy and the National Military Strategy. Do TSC exercises or implementation of FDOs constitute coordinated containment actions, or are they more related to general deterrence, simple training in international arenas, or are they something else entirely?

Research Question

This thesis focuses on answering one main question: does a correlation exist between Cold War containment principles and today's foreign policies dealing with non-super power entities, including non-state actors such as terrorist organizations and their sponsor countries?

Methodology Summary

The qualitative case study method dominates the thesis, though it occasionally makes use of other research styles when germane. Understanding the political situation from the point of view of the presidents and policy advisors who designed and implemented containment policies is critical to analyzing the phenomenon of containment itself. A phenomenological study would therefore be appropriate, but

5

because no unstructured personal interviews were conducted, this method was excluded. Instead, content analysis of historical accounts extracted key components, both constants and variables, to build a representative model to illustrate how containment works.[5]

Assumptions

1. Although containment remains non-codified in military doctrine as a defined mission, particularly at the strategic level, it has, and some would argue continues, to rely heavily upon military "muscle" to provide the crucial credibility and capability components associated with the deterrence elements of a containment strategy. Therefore, military professionals must understand the theories of how containment works, as well as broader deterrence, in order to offer their best-informed military advice.

2. Containment, because of its reliance on deterrence, cannot be completely understood without a thorough understanding of deterrence principles themselves.

3. Deterrence is one goal of containment, though not the only one. Others could include encouragement to pursue alternate courses of action, maintenance of status quo, or outright capitulation, though obviously never labeled as such.

4. Formulation of a single set of containment elements that fits all national security strategy situations, though desirable and simplifying is not possible due to an almost infinite number of variables. Each situation is different, and though prudent to consult historical examples, every application of deterrent efforts, including containment strategies, requires unique lines of operation.

Limits/Exclusions

Understanding Cold War history is critical to understanding how containment policies evolved, but because this thesis primarily addresses current applicability of containment, this thesis purposely limits variation in historical viewpoints considered. chapter 3 explains this limitation in further detail.

The thesis limits its study of post-Cold War cases to Somalia from 1993 to the present day. The many other available post-Cold War cases necessitate further analysis, and remain an acknowledged limitation.

Another self-imposed thesis limitation is its lack of emphasis on quantifiable analysis. For instance, though many budgetary information tables were available for analytical comparison between various levels of political administrations' financial commitment to different containment case studies, the thesis primarily relies on qualitative analysis instead. Statistics, though conceivably useful, remain virtually ignored.

Definitions

While the Department of Defense and North Atlantic Treaty Organization (NATO) do not define containment, they do agree on the definition of its root, contain.

Contain. ―To stop, hold, or surround the forces of the enemy or to cause the enemy to center activity on a given front and to prevent the withdrawal of any part of the enemy's force for use elsewhere."[6]

Containment. A coordinated national level policy originally designed post WWII to keep the Soviet Union from extending its sphere of influence beyond its 1947 boundaries. Current use of the term often describes a foreign policy designed to prevent a

7

targeted country, proxy organization, or terrorist group from conducting military operations or spreading its influence outside their borders or defined operating area. Containment policy typically uses varied doses of diplomacy, information, military action, and economic policy (DIME) as levers to achieve desired results.

Deterrence. Joint Publication 5-0 defines deterrence as "The prevention from action by fear of the consequences. Deterrence is a state of mind brought about by the existence of a credible threat of unacceptable counteraction."[7]

For the purposes of this thesis, deterrence is accomplished when the threat components of a country's actual Capability multiplied by its perceived Credibility result in a product deemed sufficient by the target entity's psyche to prevent an otherwise planned action from occurring. The following mathematical expression further simplifies this: Capability x Credibility = Deterrence.

Deterrence Operations Objectives. ―To decisively influence the adversary's decision-making calculus in order to prevent hostile actions against U.S. vital interests."[8]

Dissuasion. The combined efforts of military and other instruments of national power resulting in the persuasion of the enemy to not attempt to acquire or bolster a capability perceived to be threatening in nature.

Preemption. ―To strike first (or attempt to do so) in the face of an attack that is either already underway or is very credibly imminent."[9] Note: Often misinterpreted as prevention, possibly due to its misuse as stated in the Bush Doctrine. More detail follows in chapter 2.

Prevention. A conscious choice by an entity to ―launch military action, because of its fears for the future should it fail to act now."[10]

Strategy. ―The process by which ends are related to means, intentions to capabilities, objectives to resources."[11]

Deterrence through Containment

Key documents and policies discussing how the concepts of deterrence fit into the overall strategy of containment were developed and implemented throughout the Cold War. They included the writings and enduring influence of George Kennan (who originally coined the term containment), the now-declassified National Security Council Report 68 (NSC-68) approved and implemented by the Truman Administration, the New Look (Massive Retaliation) policy of the Eisenhower Administration, the Flexible Response policy of the Kennedy Administration, and the Détente Policy first created and implemented by the Nixon Administration, but left largely in place until the 1979 Soviet invasion of Afghanistan. President Carter, alarmed by the possibility that the Soviets would be able to gain access and control of Middle East oil resources (via Afghanistan and then through Iran), announced a policy, later dubbed the Carter Doctrine, that promised to defend U.S. interests in the Persian Gulf. Reagan's Peace Through Strength strategy (or Reagan Doctrine) evolved from the improving relations with the Soviet Union following their withdrawal from Afghanistan.[12]

Two Containment Philosophies: Symmetrical and Asymmetrical

Cold War Containment theorists and practitioners agreed on two common and simultaneous larger objectives: simultaneously avoid the extremes of war and the consequences of appeasement.[13] Though U.S. presidential administrations from Truman through Reagan subscribed to various versions of containment when considering the

Soviet Union, two general philosophical camps evolved from Kennan's initial containment concept: Symmetrical and Asymmetrical Containment.

Symmetrical Containment, as contained within the precepts of NSC-68, was a philosophy that meant that all U.S. interests were vital, all threats were dangerous, and therefore the country's policy would be to use all available resources to counter them. Typically and historically, this was a Democratic stance, though the Carter Administration distanced itself from it.

Asymmetrical Containment was a philosophy that recognized that resources were finite and therefore could not be equally, if at all, applied against all threats to U.S. interests. Like the reciprocal of Symmetrical Containment adherents, Asymmetrical Containment advocates tended to be Republican, though Reagan's strong moral convictions convincing him of the universal evils of communism put him more in the Symmetric camp.

Those advocating symmetrical containment believed it was the morally responsible stance to take because it committed the U.S. to respond to every situation that threatened its interests and democratic ideology. There was no distinction between allowing a country to fall under communist domination in an area outside the traditional U.S. sphere of influence, such as Korea or Vietnam, versus a country in its own backyard, such as Cuba. The policy provided protection against letting a relatively minor situation escalate into a major crisis because it obligated some level of response before getting that far. The decision to commit at least some resources to the problem was predetermined.

In contrast, asymmetrical containment advocates pointed out that the U.S. could not possibly respond to every global situation, nor should it. It required our leadership to distinguish rationally, even cold-bloodedly, between peripheral and vital interests, tolerable and intolerable threats, feasible and unfeasible responses."[14] Asymmetrical containment jeopardizes Just War principles (further discussed in chapter 2) and moral governance, despite its more realistic outlook. Another disadvantage to asymmetrical containment, Kissinger and Nixon among its major proponents, is that it sometimes draws criticism as being nothing more than cleverly disguised appeasement.

Possible Reasons for Lack of Deterrence Planning within Military

Military doctrinal publications address the value of deterrence, though not the specific strategy of containment. Joint Publication 3-0 states, "An early analysis and assessment of the adversary's decision-making process must be performed to know what actions will be an effective deterrent." Confusion however regarding deterrence's overall importance to military actions emanates from the same publication's next sentence: "Emphasis should be placed on setting the conditions for successful joint operations in the "dominate" and follow-on phases."[15] This sequencing implies that the dominating phase, which usually involves traditional lethal operations, requires the preponderance of military planning, at the expense of deterrence planning. The phrase "if deterrence fails" typically found in military planning documents often causes the assumption that the deterrence efforts "will" fail, and therefore not much time is spent trying to plan or implement it. Of course, because any given containment strategy, or individual deterrence action is extremely difficult to predict whether it will be successful, it is prudent to plan for its possible failure. Another reason why deterrence planning may not get much attention could be due to the assumption that the military has traditionally held a limited role in that arena, with the bulk of the planning previously deferred to the State Department or another government agency or department.

If an actual shooting war commences, the previous deterrence efforts rightly wear the ―failed" label. This, without doubt, reshapes the warfighter's mindset into focusing on winning the current battle. Educating the military about deterrence's potential value ―during" the fight, to include ways to reduce escalation or ways to channel the conflict into a shorter time span, may sufficiently elevate deterrence concepts in their minds to achieve the co-equal status envisioned by the Joint Service documents.

Lawrence Freedman, in the introduction to his book *Deterrence*, characterizes his subject as ―a policy reliant on threats rather than inducements, and stressing military issues above the political and economic."[16] While the latter two discipline's roles are debatable within deterrence, because political and economic threats are critical as well, Freedman's statement nonetheless holds water with the first part. A threat, by definition does not convey an actual carried out action. Rather, it merely suggests or promises such action if the deterring nation fails to get compliance with whatever its demands are. Inducements, on the other hand, are synonymous with appeasement, which, as history has illustrated on more than one occasion, seldom achieves the desired long-term result unless coupled with a deterrence component. In other words, the appeasement carrot has a better chance of working if accompanied by a credible deterrent stick.

The word ―appeasement" has a negative connotation, at least to the Western ear, due in no small part to the disastrous policy pursued by British Prime Minister Neville Chamberlain toward Adolph Hitler. Had Chamberlain attached a credible deterrent package of consequences to his appeasement pledge, with the promise to invoke if broken

12

by the other party however, the policy may have had a better chance of success. It would be interesting to study if renaming "appeasement" to something slightly less pejorative, like "accommodation" or perhaps "negotiated concessions" would render the action more palatable to military and civilian leadership.

Deterrence on its own is a policy that rests somewhat precariously between one of aggression (instilling fear) and appeasement (capitulating cooperation). This is because deterrence contains both a promise of pain and a promise of reward, depending on the targeted entity's response. Throughout a typical military doctrinal manual, a reader will find examples of the merits of "seizing the initiative" or other aggressive actions such as "dominating activities," along with two phases (II & III) to deal exclusively with them. The Deter phase (I) is mentioned, and flexible deterrent options are included briefly, but the overall emphasis observed in doctrinal discussions remains firmly focused on lethal operations. This lack of focus on deterrence and little to no discussion of containment may reflect that doctrinal manuals have not caught up yet with the Naval Operations Concept and the Army's Operating Concept.

Another plausible reason specific containment or even general deterrence gets little emphasis is due to its never-ending nature and difficulty to achieve a sense of accomplishment. Notoriously challenging measures of effectiveness compound the issue. How does one know if a containment policy was successful "because" of the policy, or was the desired result achieved from some unrelated reason? The target of containment may have chosen a course of action compatible with its implementing country for totally unrelated reasons. It is not easy to spark enthusiasm for a policy or planning process that cannot promise tangible and exclusive results. Freedman continues this line of reasoning

13

by pointing out that "successful deterrence, marked by nothing much happening, is unlikely to get the pulse racing. It has no natural constituency."[17] There are no "Deterrence Now" T-shirts, posters, or deterrence advocate groups of people at political rallies. Like the colloquial media criticism, a policy of deterrence does not "bleed" and therefore it is unlikely to "lead" any news broadcasts. Yet, the current national and military guidance remains that it is as important to prevent wars, as it is to win them. Craft a policy to elevate the prestige associated with deterrence planning to an equal plane with traditional military operations, and the Joint Chiefs' vision has a chance to succeed.

Why Pursue a Policy of Deterrence?

The deterrence term, defined earlier and briefly discussed, still requires a purpose and justification for conducting deterrence operations. It all boils down to two basic principles, though of course they all have many branches:

Principle One: To preserve a country's limited resources (blood & treasure)

Principle Two: To honor and uphold a country or a society's morals, principles, and traditions, as well as to elevate the country's global prestige and leadership role

The prestige and leadership components of Principle Two can sometimes function as sole motivation, but rarely publically admitted, even if it is obviously true.

A famous example that some would argue covers both principles is the debate about the death penalty. Some people believe that the deterrent effect of carrying out the sentence of a capital crime will compel potential criminals to reconsider the actions that may earn them the same fate. The death penalty is thus justified because it will result in fewer capital crimes (Principle One, with treasure in this case represented by potential

14

future victims being spared). Others make the case that the just punishment for willfully murdering another citizen (or some other offense deemed worthy of the death penalty) is state-administered execution, as "an eye-for-an-eye" approach. This treatment is not necessarily concerned with preventing others from emulating similar criminal behavior; rather it is seen as an appropriate punishment for a heinous crime, and happily also incidentally an effective and permanent way to eliminate the future threat from that particular individual to any other citizen: Principle Two, which in this case is upholding a society's values.

Somalia in 1991-1993 is a useful military case study that can illustrate Principle Two. Though there were no compelling national interest motivations at the time for the U.S. to intervene in the humanitarian crisis exacerbated by Somali warlords, action was in fact taken simply because it was perceived as the right thing to do for humanitarian reasons. The current political situation of the U.S. in the early 1990s would not allow the nation to stand idly by and witness heartbreaking images on television of starving people, when it had the resources available and a public mandate to make a tangible difference. Aside from the immediate relief efforts, the intended deterrence message to Mohamed Farrah Aidid and his accomplices was that the U.S. would stand up for the helpless and his kind were subject to prosecution if interfered with. As readers of history will appreciate however, adherence to Principle Two (morals) without any attached Principle One (money) motivators is ephemeral in nature, and extremely subjected to the direction of the political wind. The U.S. was unlikely to benefit financially from a stable and well-governed Somalia, and the long-term problem of piracy had not yet manifested itself. The country was, and still is, extremely poor and not a likely candidate to turn into a

15

profitable trading partner. Without a long-term financial motivator in the background, the U.S. is unlikely to commit too deeply to a purely moral "basket case" situation for an extended period.

The same Somalia case study makes this point as well when the U.S. withdrew its forces after suffering 18 KIA in the infamous scenario graphically depicted in Bowden's *Blackhawk Down*. The Somalian situation by 1993 turned from one in which the U.S. was the entity trying to deter warlords from denying food and medicine to a starving public, to one in which the U.S. itself was the one being deterred from further military actions due to the implied and demonstrated threat against continued presence.[18] An even more tragic example, also from the African continent, is the 1994 genocide in Rwanda. In this case, approximately 800,000 people were murdered in 100 days simply for belonging to the "wrong" ethnic group. Racial favoritism of Tutsis by Belgian colonists left lingering resentment by the majority Hutus, and a series of events, culminated by President Habyarimana's (a Hutu) aircraft being shot down by a man-portable surface-to-air missile. This triggered cascading and brutal retribution by the Hutus on Tutsis leading to the Rwandan Genocide, as it is known today.[19] Gun shy from the aftereffects of the Somalia experience a year earlier, and again lacking compelling monetary interests in the region, the U.S. did not actively leverage its military to stop the carnage in Rwanda, despite its longstanding moral principles.

Objective vs. Subjective Evaluations of Deterrence Effectiveness

Proving the effectiveness of a containment effort or deterrence action is difficult, if not impossible. It is usually fairly obvious when deterrence fails, but when it works, how does one actually know that it was a direct or causal result of the deterrence policy itself rather than a host of other factors? This does not mean those efforts should be abandoned however. Credit goes to David Ogilvy, the famous advertising executive, with admitting that ―99 percent of advertising doesn't sell much of anything,‖ but he still strongly advocated advertising as a crucial component of anyone's successful business plan.[20] Ogilvy at least was occasionally able to ask customers directly through surveys or other methods why they chose a certain product, and whether that decision related to his advertising campaigns. A terrorist organization is unlikely to admit via survey or any other collection method that it refrained from conducting operations against a specific target because it was worried about retaliation from a deterring counterforce. Deterrence, like advertising, is a mixture of art and science, and therefore cannot always be perfectly measureable in effectiveness. Often both will fail to achieve their goals outright, or will take longer than originally anticipated. When they are successful however, that success can be priceless. Those successes justify the continuing efforts in each discipline to improve the overall processes. The art component of containment strategy or deterrence actions contains an almost endless list of variables, which makes every situation unique. The more concrete science component of deterrence action however implies that there may be certain constants, which if discovered and exploited, could aid in the planner's processes. Lacking these, evaluation methods for deterrence effectiveness are often limited to anecdotal examples, and caution therefore is called for when analyzing various deterrence theory practices.

In summary, this paper explores the evolution of U.S. containment policy from its origins as an answer against Soviet expansion efforts immediately following WWII, and tracks its changes throughout the following Cold War. Next, it collects and analyzes

17

various war theories and foreign policy theories to determine how various philosophies affect the decision making process of civilian policy makers. It then analyzes the post-Cold War case study of Somalia for possible present day residual application of containment theory. Its conclusions state that prudent formulation of containment using tried-and-true lessons from the Cold War contain the potential for successful foreign policy against non-state entities such as terrorist organizations. Though remaining outside this thesis study, the conclusion suggests a coordinated and coherent containment foreign policy may enjoy long-term success against ascending powers like China, and lesser powers, including Iran, North Korea, and Venezuela as well.

---

[1]U.S. Marine Corps, U.S. Navy, and U.S. Coast Guard, *Naval Operations Concept 2010* (Washington, DC: Department of Defense, 2009), 2.

[2]Ibid.

[3]U.S. Army, *Operating Concept 2016-2028 Version 2.0* (Washington, DC: Department of Defense, 2010), iii.

[4]John L. Gaddis, *Strategies of Containment* (New York, NY: Oxford University Press, 1982), 329.

[5]Paul D. Leedy and Jeanne E. Ormrod, *Practical Research Planning and Design* 8th ed. (Upper Saddle River, NJ: Pearson Education, Inc., 2005), 139.

[6]U.S. Army, Field Manual (FM) 1-02, *Operational Terms and Graphics* (Washington DC: Department of the Army, 2010), 1-43.

[7]Department of Defense, Joint Publication 5-0, *Joint Operation Planning* (Washington DC: Department of the Army, 2010), GL-11.

[8]Department of Defense, *Deterrence Operations Joint Operating Concept Version 2.0.* (Offutt Air Force Base, NE: U.S. Strategic Command, 2006), 5.

[9]Colin S. Gray, ―The Implications of Preemptive and Preventive War Doctrines: A Reconsideration" (Monograph, Strategic Studies Institute, Carlisle Barracks, PA, 2007), 5.

[10]Ibid.

[11]Gaddis, *Strategies of Containment,* viii.

[12]Gaddis, *Strategies of Containment,* Chapters 2-11.

[13]Ibid., 388.

[14]Ibid., 343.

[15]Department of Defense, Joint Publication 3-0, *Joint Operations Incorporating Change 1* (Washington DC: Joint Chiefs of Staff, 2006 with change 1 in 2008), V-4.

[16]Lawrence Freedman, *Deterrence* (Cambridge, UK: Polity Press, 2004), 1.

[17]Ibid.

[18]Mark Bowden, *Black Hawk Down* (New York, NY: Signet Books, 1999), 426-27.

[19]BBC News, ‒Rwanda: How the Genocide Happened," 18 December 2008, http://news.bbc.co.uk/2/hi/africa/1288230.stm (accessed 22 February 2011).

[20]John Jantsch, ‒99% of Advertising Doesn't Sell a Thing," *Duct Tape Marketing*, 14 May 2006, http://www.ducttapemarketing.com/blog/2006/05/14/99-of-advertising-doesnt-sell-a-thing/ (accessed 25 October 2010).

CHAPTER 2

LITERATURE REVIEW

This thesis explores how U.S. containment strategy evolved throughout the Cold War and whether those historical examples contain relevancy toward modern policies directed against non-superpower targets, with special focus on non-state actors and terrorist organizations. The thesis accomplishes this by dividing into three major sections: (1) containment policies of Cold War administrations, (2) war and foreign policy theories, and (3) post-Cold War non-state case studies.

To facilitate the literature review, each major section further subdivides into three categories: (1) books, (2) U.S. government documents and publications, and (3) scholarly journal articles and other sources. All studied materials were unclassified or declassified documents.

Books

Various criteria this thesis used to select books to consult include:

1. The prominence of author in his or her field

2. Additional authors' concurring or dissenting opinions

3. The logic of stance or argument

Government Publications

Selection criteria this thesis used to chose government publications to consult for this section include:

1. Authority of particular document. For instance, a Presidential National Security Strategy contains considerably more authority than an individual service's doctrinal manual.

2. Relevance to subject. Often a lower echelon document contains more relevancy than a wider aperture national paper.

3. Common starting point. Due to their public nature, government publications provide orientation references from which other discussions can then originate.

Scholarly Journal Articles and Other Sources

Like the previous categories, this thesis chose various scholarly journal articles, monographs, speeches, interviews, and studies for a variety of purposes including:

1. Subject matter experts often write relevant articles outside normal book publishing routes, and their opinions frequently shape political decision makers' policy formulation. Their contents therefore merit consideration and inclusion in overall analysis.

2. Bloggers, film producers, and others with access to public media outlets often shape public opinion, regardless of their specific or demonstrated expertise in given subject areas. Public policy can be affected as a result, and therefore occasional consideration of their arguments becomes necessary.

Part 1: U.S. Cold War Containment Policies

Part 1(Books)

Part 1 of the literature review, Cold War Containment Policies, relies heavily on the works of noted Cold War historian and Yale University professor of Military and

Naval history, John L. Gaddis. It deviates from standard opinion "compare and contrast" models for reasons more fully explained in chapter 3's methodology. Historical events, ideas, concepts, and opinions from Gaddis' quintessential *Strategies of Containment* from 1982, and his more recent book *The Cold War: A New History*, comprise the bulk of Part 1's contents.

Part 1 (Government Documents)

Part 1 addresses historical events and policies, and as mentioned earlier, books by John Gaddis dominate this section. Gaddis cites multiple government documents and speeches, including key National Security Council findings, embassy cables by State Department employee George F. Kennan, and Presidential inaugural or State of the Union addresses.

Additionally, the thesis used a declassified National Security Council memorandum, which summarizes President Eisenhower's Project Solarium.

Chapter 1's introduction uses many government publications and documents including the National Security Strategy (multiple years), Department of Defense Joint Publications 3-0 and 5-0, U.S. Army Field Manual 1-02, Army Operating Concept 2016-2028 Version 2.0, and the USMC, USN, and USCG's Naval Operations Concept 2010.

Part 1 (Scholarly Journal Articles and Other Sources)

George Kennan, though an employee of the State Department, published his "X" article in the influential civilian journal *Foreign Affairs*, and it had a dramatic effect on U.S. foreign policy.

W.B. Pickett edited a monograph entitled ―George F. Kennan and the Origins of Eisenhower‘s New Look: an Oral History of Project Solarium.‖

Part 1: Synopsis of U.S. Cold War Containment Policy Evolution

Historian John L. Gaddis methodically works the reader from the Cold War‘s origins, through the initial development of containment strategy, and continues explaining how containment evolved during the different Presidential Administrations. The thesis took Gaddis‘s insights, analyzed them using the next chapter‘s methodology, and presented the results in chapter 4.

Kennan‘s Role and Influence

George F. Kennan, then a State Department expert on the Soviet Union when his work was recognized, played an enormous role in influencing U.S. containment strategy throughout the Cold War. Kennan, then stationed at the American Embassy in Moscow, was given the task of assessing reasons why the Soviet Union behaved as it did, and why the Grand Alliance of WWII seemed doomed. Kennan‘s now famous, hastily written reply, came in the form of an 8,000–word cable, and was sent via telegram to Washington on 22 February 1946. This telegram, along with an additional expansion published anonymously in Foreign Affairs, formed the backbone of U.S. containment strategy toward the Soviet Union for the remainder of the Cold War.[1]

Kennan‘s Assessment of Moscow‘s Basic Nature

1. Moscow‘s obstinacy was not driven by Western actions; rather the outside
   world was treated as hostile by Soviets because it provided the only excuse

‑for the dictatorship without which they did not know how to rule, for cruelties they did not dare not to inflict, for sacrifices they felt bound to demand."[2]

2. It was naïve to expect Western diplomatic concessions be reciprocated by Moscow.

3. Moscow strategy had little chance for dramatic change until a future leader (well beyond Stalin) realized enough policy failures and implemented a change.

4. War was not required (though remained possible) to achieve positive change in Moscow. Instead, Kennan articulated a policy of ‑long-term patient but firm and vigilant ‑containment" of Russian expansive tendencies."[3] (emphasis added)

Kennan's Policy Advice

Kennan's rapid rise to diplomatic stardom led to his advice to politicians for dealing with the Soviets. Applicability of certain suggestions beyond this Cold War superpower remains possible.

1. Make disagreements open, but non-provocative

2. No concessions, but allow current possessions to stand

3. Increase military and extend economic and military aid to allies

4. Continue negotiating, but limit goals to gaining acknowledgement of U.S. positions and to gain additional allies abroad

5. Project the image that the U.S. is ‑too strong to be beaten, and too determined to be frightened."[4]

24

Truman Doctrine and NSC-68

President Truman, in his famous speech on March 12, 1947 addressing Soviet expansion aims in Turkey and Greece proclaimed that, "it must be the policy of the U.S. to support free peoples who are resisting attempted subjugation by armed minorities or outside pressures."[5] This policy, known as the "Truman Doctrine," formally codified in NSC-68, established the U.S. policy of containment against the Soviet Union. Kennan's influence remained undeniable, though Truman's policy theoretically applied universally (symmetrically), while Kennan did not advocate equally helping everyone under threat of Communist expansion.[6]

Eisenhower's New Look (Massive Retaliation)

Key members of President Eisenhower's administration, including his Secretary of State John Foster Dulles, urged the President to "roll back" or "liberate" countries that had fallen under Soviet control or domination. Eisenhower however, wary of provoking new wars and incurring unsustainable economic debt, and concerned that Truman's containment policies were flawed, directed a new look at what his policy should be.[7]

Project Solarium, so-named due to the 3rd floor location in the White House where it was discussed, became the method Eisenhower used to construct his foreign policy concerning containment of Communist expansion. Its conclusions, again strongly influenced by Kennan's input and analysis, steered Eisenhower's policy toward a more asymmetric form of containment. More importantly, Eisenhower's actions established containment, even though not identical to Truman's version, as basically non-partisan in nature. Various iterations of containment policy followed throughout the remainder of the Cold War, and yielded many components, further analyzed in chapter 4.[8]

Kennedy's Flexible Response

President Kennedy realized that technological developments in nuclear weaponry's accuracy and potential yields made them too powerful to threaten their use, unless in the most dire circumstances. He therefore attempted to institutionalize the notion of limited war, including limited nuclear war, with a new doctrine: Flexible Response"[9]

Important developments of Flexible Response included:

1. The creation of escalatory steps to be taken, starting with conventional limited responses, and eventually leading to nuclear response, if the Soviets failed to stop unacceptable operations.[10]

2. The concept of Mutually Assured Destruction (MAD), which espoused the idea that one's population could best be protected by leaving it vulnerable, so long as the other side face comparable vulnerabilities."[11]

3. The use of ambiguity and unpredictability as a deterrent virtue. Walt Rostow, one of Kennedy's national security advisors, wrote, We wish to assure them (U.S.S.R.) that we do not intend to strike them first if they do not transgress the frontiers of the free community, but that we might well strike first under certain circumstances if they do."[12]

Johnson's Continuation of Flexible Response

President Johnson, for the most part, continued Kennedy's containment policy, and emphasized that surrender anywhere threatens defeat everywhere."[13] Johnson and Kennedy, therefore swung U.S. policy back to the symmetric camp, but remained vaguer than Truman with what exactly merited containment, and which method was to be used.[14]

Nixon's Détente

President Nixon and his closest foreign policy advisor, Henry Kissinger, constructed a highly complex containment strategy that no longer believed that global power was a ―zero sum game.‖ ―It was the overall calculus of power that was important, not the defeats or victories that might take place in isolated theaters of competition‖[15] Important strategic changes implemented under the Nixon-Kissinger watch included:

1. Cessation of effort to impose American-style democracy on other societies[16]

2. Changed defense policy from one of maintaining superiority, to one that maintained sufficient deterrence capability against the Soviet Union[17]

3. Took full advantage of the growing Sino-Soviet schism[18]

Ford's Continuation of Détente

President Ford's retention of Henry Kissinger as Secretary of State ensured his basic foreign policy toward the Kremlin would be very similar to Nixon's. While Ford's version of détente and asymmetric containment remained intact, he occasionally became involved in smaller, more symmetric-like, foreign interventions, including Angola and Chile.[19]

Carter Doctrine

President Carter, in an effort to distinguish his foreign policies with his predecessors, instead ended up creating confusion among his own advisors and the Soviets he was trying to contain. He simultaneously emphasized human rights issues, while keeping Republican approaches of differentiating between vital and peripheral interests and working with some communists to contain others.[20] Carter's contradictory policies were pursued in an attempt to ─win the support of critics on the Right who had objected to Kissinger's _appeasement' of the Soviet Union, and those on the Left who had worried about his _amorality'"[21]

Reagan's Peace through Strength

President Reagan's foreign policy, unlike other Republican administrations, favored the symmetrical mindset, though he astutely avoided the traps of becoming involved in every situation this policy would typically call for. Additional deviations from conventional thinking included:

1. Long-term reliance on nuclear weapons to preserve peace would eventually lead to nuclear war. He thus rejected concepts of MAD and the Strategic Arms Limitation Talks (SALT) process.

2. Detente, as a policy, failed to offer hope of a solution . . . rather it had frozen it in place.[22]

3. Rather than limit nuclear weapons, Reagan wanted to reduce them, and therefore proposed the Strategic Arms Reduction Talks (START).

4. His was the first presidency to frame its Soviet containment strategy in a way that would deliberately target Soviet weaknesses, rather than try to counter their strengths.[23]

Chapter 4 presents containment strategy analysis of President Truman through President Reagan, with applicability comparisons to contemporary non-state situations.

Part 2: War and Foreign Policy Theories

Part 2 (Books)

Books provided the dominant resource for Part 2's consideration of various war, foreign policy, deterrence, and containment theories.

Selected authors include University of Chicago Political Scientist Professor John J. Mearsheimer, Columbia University International Relations Professor and neorealist Kenneth Waltz, retired Princeton Social Science Professor Michael Walzer, Harvard Law School Professor Alan Dershowitz, documentary film producer Eugene Jarecki, Cold War strategist Herman Kahn, and Professor of War Studies at King's College in London, Sir Lawrence Freedman.

Part 2 (Government Documents)

Part 2 concerns itself primarily with theory, and as such relies mostly on non-government sources from university professors, think tanks, and the like. Major exceptions however include President Bush's *2002 National Security Strategy* discussing preemption, and U.S. Strategic Command's *Deterrence Operations Joint Operating Concept Version 2.0.*

Part 2 (Scholarly Journal Articles and Other Sources)

Key journal articles and monographs for Part 2's theory discussions included George Washington University professor of Political Science and International Affairs, Charles L. Glasser, and University of Reading, England professor of International Politics and Strategic Studies, Colin S. Gray. Their works contributed to better understanding of realism theory and preemptive/preventive policies, respectively.

Part 2: Synopsis of War and Foreign Policy Theories

The second part of this literature review, like the first part, considers sources ranging from official government documents and political speeches, to contemporary and historical books, as well as scholarly journal articles. This section differs from the first though with its focus on a selected variety of foreign policy theories, their development and application, and implementation.

Foreign Policy Theory: Important or Not?

Not all policy makers subscribe to the idea that adhering to certain theories over others in day-to-day policy formation is a laudable goal. Paul Nitze, the principle author of President Truman's NSC-68, actually felt that most conventional political theory written and taught since WWII either detracts from, or has limited value in producing actual policy.[24]

University of Chicago Political Science Professor John J. Mearsheimer however feels that politicians must choose a framework as a starting point upon which they can formulate their foreign policy. He admits that theories are necessarily simple, and thus ignore certain variables, while emphasizing the perceived main or causal factors for a given situation or condition. That being said, he still strongly believes politicians who proceed without any fundamental understanding of how the world works will likely see their policies fail or suffer from unintended and unanticipated second and third order effects.[25]

Liberal Foreign Policy Theories

The following statements, according to Mearsheimer, shape conventional thinking and drive much of deterrence policy options and containment strategy planning efforts:

1. Prosperous states that share intertwined economic interests are unlikely to fight each other.

2. Sufficiently democratic states do not fight each other.

3. International institutions build cooperative relationships while helping states avoid war.[26]

Realism Variants

Defensive Realism: Prominent proponents include theorists such as Kenneth Waltz and Charles Glaser. This theory advocates the belief that a sufficient defensive capability provides adequate national security. While often focused on nuclear and other Weapons of Mass Destruction (WMD) threats, and the need to establish and maintain a viable second-strike capability, defensive realism also includes accommodations for defensive capabilities against terrorism and attacks of a more conventional nature.[27]

Offensive Realism: Mearsheimer argues against the conventional wisdom of liberal foreign theory previously listed. He believes that anarchy and the distribution of power are the factors that matter most for explaining international politics, and thus best used as predictors of a country or non-state actor's future behavior. He feels countries will naturally seek regional hegemony, regardless of the conventional beliefs listed above. Democracies may be nice; economic interdependence creates some bonds; international institutions like the United Nations or other regional organizations may promote some positive behavior; yet all these statements are insufficient to deter a country's natural tendency to consolidate its regional dominance and then prevent anyone else from interfering with its status.[28]

Just War Theory

American politicians, particularly those ascending to the highest office of the land, tend to incorporate varying applications of Just War theory into their decision making process. Regardless of their previous propensities to side with doves or hawks, the President, as Commander in Chief, wields the power and responsibility to protect the citizens from all enemies, foreign or domestic. This reality drives Presidents to justify their actions, particularly lethal military or economic in nature, using Just War principles.

Well known Just War theorist and retired Social Science professor from Princeton, Michael Walzer writes that though he is predisposed against militarily intervention, he realizes war is sometimes justifiable. In the same breath however, he states that war will always be subject to moral criticism.[29] He believes that any war designed to expand territory or influence, or to improve economic standing are unjust. Examples of Just wars however include actions designed to prevent ethnic cleansing.

Just War theory balances a leader's responsibility to act in the interests of his nation, while not wrongly harming another nation. Walzer objectively defines National Interest as present power and wealth plus the probability of future power and wealth.[30] A nation's interest does not necessarily align morally with Just War principles, because obtaining that ―future power and wealth" may illegally or immorally harm the nation or people currently possessing it.

Just War Critiques and Responses

Critique 1: Just War uses morals to make war easier to fight.

Response 1: War is always terrible, and will cause harm to innocents as well as belligerents, but some situations still morally (justly) demand lethal action. Examples include Nazi Germany as a justly fought war, and Rwanda's 1994 genocide as a just cause missed opportunity.[31]

Critique 2: Just War proponents frame war on issues before war commences, instead of considering broader motivations like imperialism, resource grabs, and power.

Response 2: Expand criticism to include these broader motivations.[32]

Preemption vs. Prevention

President George W. Bush's National Security Strategy, published in 2002, interchangeably used the words preemption and prevention.[33] This confusion lingers today, with reflections in a considerable range of literature including academic articles, governmental policy statements, and editorials continuing to substitute the word preemption, when prevention is more accurate. For purposes of this thesis, Dr. Colin S. Gray's definitions of preemption and prevention are used, and the author with brackets to avoid confusion, will correct quotes from sources incorrectly using terminology.

Preemption, used properly is never controversial, while preventive policy is always controversial. ―Preempt means to strike first (or attempt to do so) in the face of an attack that is either already underway or is very credibly imminent."[34] It can therefore be considered a form of internationally recognized self-defense. Prevention on the other hand is discretionary. The preventor chooses war or military action because of perceived future threats that would be more difficult to handle if left to fester.[35] Under certain circumstances, Gray sees no issue with a state using preventive measures against another state or non-state terrorist organization, but concedes such measures will remain controversial.

Alan Dershowitz concurs with Gray that preventive policy is occasionally justified, and agrees that many will never agree with this course of action. His book, *Preemption: A Knife that Cuts Both Ways*, points out that if prevention were successfully executed, neither the preventor nor the rest of the world ever know the extent of what exactly was prevented. This point underscores the problems with deterrence and containment, in that a lack of conflict or broader war cannot be proven to be the result of the preventive, deterrent, or containment efforts.[36]

Robert Pape disagrees, and stated, ―Preventive war by the U.S. would violate one of the most important norms of international politics―that democracies do not fight preventive wars.‖[37] Just because Pape‗s statement, made prior to the U.S. invasion of Iraq, reflected accurate history, it does not follow that the U.S. should ―never‖ fight a preventive war. As the example of WWII shows, an argument can easily be made that the U.S. ―should‖ have fought a preventive war, despite the Pape-cited ―norms of international politics.‖

Princeton professor Richard Falk echoed Pape‗s comments when criticizing U.S. Iraq policy by lamenting the lack of accountability to the United Nations or ―dependence on a collective judgment of responsible governments‖ before committing to military action.[38]

Both Pape and Falk, unlike Gray, seem to advocate that demonstrating legitimacy and conformance with international expectations and norms trumps the perceived national security and sovereignty of the U.S.

Harvard's Kennedy School of Government created a National Security Program report in 1997 that listed five key intelligence components that must be analyzed and fused into a cohesive picture before decision makers can determine if/when either preemptive or preventive action can justifiably be taken:

The convergence in time and space of an adversary's

1. Capability

2. Intention

3. Past History

4. Opportunity

5. Current Actions[39]

Deterrence and Containment Theory

The Department of Defense (DoD) contradicts itself frequently both with what it chooses to publish, and with what it either fails to publish, or fails to update or deconflict with its other publications. No service field manual or joint publication yet exists dedicated to conflict prevention, even while various services' operating concepts agree that conflict prevention shares coequal status to that of fighting and winning the nation's wars. The DoD has delegated authorship of the Deterrence Operations Joint Operating Concept to the U.S. Strategic Command, but the document is past due for updating, and has not been elevated to Joint Publication status. DoD publications, for all its faults, retains relevancy however, and provides useful definitions, concepts, and goals for this thesis. STRATCOM's DOJOC, for example, though outdated, provides the most accessible and succinct treatment of deterrence the thesis research has discovered.[40]

Prominent Cold War strategist Herman Kahn's works focused primarily on nuclear war with the Soviet Union. His writings influenced many planners to work out situations where nuclear war could actually be winnable, and thus moved past mere containment. Paradoxically, this line of thought contributed to containment's effectiveness, because it convinced many leaders that total disarmament was the only way to prevent global destruction.[41] Conventional wisdom postulates the terrorism phenomenon is a constant, and cannot be eradicated, only defended against. Kahn's work remains applicable, if just for the fact that his belief a nuclear war was winnable, could be extrapolated today that a properly formed and executed containment policy can ―win" the terrorism fight.

Sir Lawrence Freedman believes in the whole of government approach to deterrence strategy, but feels it rests more heavily on the military aspect than the levers of diplomacy. He believes, like Machiavelli's Prince, that it is better to be feared than loved.[42]

Part 3: Post-Cold War Non-State Case Studies

Part 3 (Books)

Part 3 discusses the case studies, and various consulted books include the following authors: Senior Associate at the International Peace Academy in New York, Simon Chesterman, U.S. National War College strategy professor, Audrey Kurth Cronin, Georgetown University Security Studies professor, Paul Pillar, Director Georgetown

University's Center for Peace and Security Studies, Bruce Hoffman, and University of St Andrews in Scotland professor of International Relations, Paul Wilkinson.

Part 3 (Government Documents)

Part 3's selected literature discusses the chosen case studies, with the majority derived from non-governmental sources. Exceptions include official lessons learned and published by the National Defense University in *Somalia Operations: Lessons Learned* and official websites maintained by task forces focused on current conditions in the Horn of Africa.

Part 3 (Scholarly Journal Articles and other sources)

University of Southern California Journalism professor Philip Seib wrote about how terrorism organizations use media to get their message out, and hints at strategies that could contain them.

Naval Analysis Center researcher Daniel Whiteneck offered thoughts of how to deter terrorists, especially when conventional responses could actually bolster their overall causes.

National Defense University research fellow, M. Elain Bunn published thoughts about tailored deterrence.

Sometimes the most relevant sources for material come from areas labeled ―other." Ali Osman, an editor of the online journal *Somalilandpress.com* fits this category. One of his editorials succinctly captured his opinion of the current situation Somalia faces, as well as his prescribed fix.

Other sources for Part 3 included articles and official websites containing information about various nations' anti-piracy policies and rationales.

Part 3: Case Studies

Somalia-1993

Simon Chesterman compiled common sense lessons learned from U.S. and UN-led operations against Aideed-led Somalia in 1993:

1. Scale nation-building objectives to available resources (forces, money, will-power)

2. Complement military forces with civil capabilities (law enforcement, reconstruction, and political development)

3. Unity of effort matters just as much in peace operations as it does during war

4. Security comes before economic or political development[43]

Lawrence Freedman points out that the U.S. does not corner the market of deterrence, and in fact, deterrence has been effectively used against U.S. and United Nations (U.N.) global operations. He cites examples from the debacle in Somalia and the following year with the genocide in Rwanda.[44]

Somalia-2009

Ali Osman, an editor with the online journal *Somalilandpress.com* lists three main issues warning against current U.S., African Union, and U.N. plans for Somalia:

1. The Somali Transitional Government is not a reliable partner, is incompetent, and not interested in seeing the creation of a viable Somali Republic.

2. The African Union cannot maintain sufficient troops, even if they had a credible government to work with.

3. The proposed influx of 15,000 U.N. soldiers to augment African Union forces are woefully inadequate and merely represent a ―life support U.S. Containment policy." He worries about expansion of terrorist activity into Kenya, Djibouti, Ethiopia, and Uganda if al-Shabaab is temporarily pushed out of their Somalia strongholds. Because U.N. mandates are short, terrorist organizations simply wait out the authorities and return stronger than ever.

Osmans‘ solution calls for Somalis to determine their own history, and for the U.S. to simply contain terrorists within Somalia and not let them influence cross border areas.[45]

Terrorist Organizations

Professors Cronin and Pillar provide separate analysis of how terrorist organizations end, and the typical tenets of U.S. counterterrorism policy. Cronin states the six most common means that end terrorism campaigns include:

1. Decapitation: Catching or Killing the Leader

2. Negotiations: Transition toward a Legitimate Political Process

3. Achieving the Objective (tactically or strategically)

4. Failure: Imploding, Provoking a Backlash, or becoming Marginalized

5. Repression: Crushing Terrorism with Force

6. Reorientation: Transitioning to another Modus Operandi[46]

Pillar's U.S. counterterrorism list includes:

1. Make no deals or concessions to terrorists

2. Treat terrorism as a crime, and bring terrorists to justice

3. Isolate and pressure state sponsors of terrorism until their behavior changes

4. Build capability and capacity of countries friendly to U.S. counterterrorism policies[47]

Comparison of these two lists provides insight into designing future counterterrorism deterrent and containment strategies.

Philip Seib and Bruce Hoffman discuss in a separate article and book that the media can positively or negatively affect a terrorist organization's operations. It behooves the planners and policy makers to thoroughly understand the media's capabilities and limitations, and incorporate that knowledge into cohesive counterterrorism policy.[48]

Paul Wilkinson explains why democratic countries often disagree about counterterrorism courses of action:

1. Internal security and laws remain totally sovereign to individual countries.

2. Many states have yet to become victims or terrorism, and therefore do not experience the same sense of urgency as those who have.

3. Economic linkages to pro-terrorist states often prevent unified action.

4. Some states believe security can be obtained by appeasing the threatening entities.

5. Some states maintain double standards, and regard some terrorists as ―freedom fighters," as in some Irish American beliefs about the Irish Republican Army.

6. Pervasive terrorist propaganda convinces many defeatists that terrorism cannot

be defeated by democracies.[49]

Literature Review Conclusion

More than sufficient literary resources are available to pursue the answers to the

questions posed by this thesis. However, specific published works directly addressing if

or how Cold War containment theory applies to current non-state situations remain

somewhat sparse. One goal of this thesis is to partially rectify that problem. Ultimately,

the case studies require further expansion and additions, but the work included in this

thesis sheds light on the continuity of U.S. foreign policy between the Cold War and

present global situations. The next chapter explains the methodologies used to collect and

analyze the information for this thesis.

---

[1]John L. Gaddis, *The Cold War: A New History* (New York, NY: The Penguin Press, 2005), 29.

[2]John L. Gaddis, *Strategies of Containment* (New York, NY: Oxford University Press, 1982), 329.

[3]Ibid.

[4]Ibid.

[5]Ibid., 22.

[6]Ibid.

[7]W. B. Pickett, ed., ―George F. Kennan and the Origins of Eisenhower‘s New Look: an Oral History of Project Solarium" (Monograph Series Number 1, Princeton Institute for International and Regional Studies, Princeton, NJ, 2004), 2.

[8]Ibid., 9-10.

[9]Amos A. Jordan, William J. Taylor, Jr., and Michael J. Mazarr, *American National Security,* 5th ed. (Baltimore, MD: The Johns Hopkins University Press, 1999), 262.

[10]Ibid., 263.

[11]Gaddis, *Strategies of Containment*, 219.

[12]Ibid.

[13]Ibid., 210.

[14]Ibid., 212.

[15]Ibid., 275.

[16]Ibid., 276.

[17]Ibid., 278.

[18]Ibid., 282.

[19]Ibid.

[20]Ibid., 345.

[21]Ibid.

[22]Gaddis, *The Cold War*, 357.

[23]Ibid., 355.

[24]John J. Mearsheimer, *The Tragedy of Great Power Politics* (New York, NY: W.W. Norton & Company, Inc., 2001), 8.

[25]Ibid., 10-11.

[26]Ibid., 9.

[27]Charles L. Glaser, ―Realists as Optimists: Cooperation as Self-Help," *International Security* 19, no. 3 (Winter 1994-1995), http://www.jstor.org/ pss/2539079 (accessed 13 March 2010), 50-90.

[28]Mearsheimer, 10-11.

²⁹Michael Walzer, *Arguing about War* (New Haven, CT: Yale University Press, 2004), ix.

³⁰Ibid., 6.

³¹Ibid., x.

³²Ibid., xi.

³³President George W. Bush, *The National Security Strategy of the United States of America September 2002* (Washington, DC: The White House, 2002), 6.

³⁴Colin S. Gray, ―The Implications of Preemptive and Preventive War Doctrines: A Reconsidation" (Monograph, Strategic Studies Institute, Carlisle Barracks, PA: 2007), v, vi.

³⁵Ibid.

³⁶Alan Dershowitz, *Preemption:A Knife that Cuts Both Ways* (New York, NY: W.W. Norton & Company, Inc., 2006), 129.

³⁷Ibid., 159.

³⁸Ibid., 161.

³⁹Ibid., 162.

⁴⁰U.S. Strategic Command, *Deterrence Operations Joint Operating Concept (DO JOC), Version 2.0* (Washington, DC: Department of Defense, 2006), 6.

⁴¹Herman Kahn, *On Thermonuclear War* (Princeton, NJ: Princeton University Press, 1960), 20.

⁴²Lawrence Freedman, ―America Needs a Wider Coalition, However Difficult," *The Independent*, 29 March 2003, http://www.independent.co.uk/opinion/commentators/lawrence-freedman-america-needs-a-wider-coalition-however-difficult-592696.html (accessed 15 January 2011).

⁴³James Dobbins, John G. McGinn, Keith Crane, Seth G. Jones, Rollie Lal, Andrew Rathmell, Rachel Swanger, and Anga Timilsina, *America's Role in Nation-Building: From Germany to Iraq* (Santa Monica, CA: RAND, 2003), 69.

⁴⁴Lawrence Freedman, *Deterrence* (Cambridge, UK: Polity Press, 2004), 125.

[45]Ali Osman, ―Op-Ed-Somalia: The Wrong Strategy" *Somalialand Press.com* http://somalilandpress.com/op-ed-somalia-the-wrong-strategy-17410 (accessed 8 March 2011).

[46]Audrey Kurth Cronin, *How Terrorism Ends: Understanding the Decline and Demise of Terrorist Campaigns* (Princeton, NJ: Princeton University Press, 2009), 13.

[47]Paul R. Pillar, *Terrorism and U.S. Foreign Policy* (Washington, DC: Brookings Institution Press, 2001), 8.

[48]Philip Seib, ―The Al-Qaeda Media Machine," *Military Review* (May-June 2008); Center for Army Lessons Learned Newsletter, No. 09-11, Ft. Leavenworth, KS, December 2008), 95; Bruce Hoffman, *Inside Terrorism* (New York, NY: Columbia University Press, 2006), 183-4.

[49]Paul Wilkinson, *Terrorism Versus Democracy* (London: Frank Cass Publishers, 2001), 222.

CHAPTER 3

METHODOLOGY

Introduction

This thesis primarily relies on the qualitative research methodology, and is applied to the following three main sections as previously discussed in chapter 2, Literature Review:

1. Cold War Presidential Administration's Containment Policies

2. Theories of war and foreign policy as related to general deterrence and specific containment principles

3. Post-Cold War non-state case studies

In order to answer the primary research question and determine whether a correlation exists between Cold War containment foreign policies and modern foreign policies focused on non-state actors and terrorist groups, sufficient background information must first be collected and analyzed.

The above-listed sections 1 and 2 performed this background collection function, and employed a simple content analysis and qualitative research methodology. Section 3, post-Cold War non-state case studies, provided the material to compare recent and current foreign policy examples against those of the Cold War. This chapter additionally covers the following topics: data collection methodology, case study selection rationale, data analysis, standards of quality and verification, and a summary.

Methodology Selection Rationale

Of the many recognized research methods, qualitative research fits best for this thesis for the selected post-Cold War case studies. Sharan Merriam, a qualitative research methodology expert and professor at the University of Georgia in Athens states that "qualitative research is an umbrella concept covering several forms of inquiry that help us understand and explain the meaning of social phenomena with as little disruption of the natural setting as possible."[1] Understanding how a carefully crafted set of deterrence principles can combine into an effective containment strategy requires just such a method.

In order for qualitative research to bear fruit, a brief use of quantitative research is required. Merriam explains: "In contrast to quantitative research, which takes apart a phenomenon to examine component parts (which become the variables of the study), qualitative research can reveal how all the parts work together to form a whole."[2] The Cold War Presidential Administration's Containment Policies section of this thesis quantitatively extracts variables and constants of containment policies for later construction of analysis matrices illustrated in chapter 4.

Similar to the historical containment policies section just described, the war and foreign policy theory section likewise identifies distinct components for inclusion in chapter 4's analysis matrices. Different presidential personalities subscribed to different philosophies, which in-turn led to variations in their foreign policies. Data collection and content analysis of these disparate theories builds overall understanding of why particular foreign policies are chosen or rejected.

The remainder of the research methodology reverts to qualitative, and attempts to discern how well those collected components work and worked as a coherent policy. As a quick example, the thesis research has revealed that Cold War containment policies usually fell into one of two quantifiable categories: symmetrical or asymmetrical. Simply analyzing these two variables alone however is insufficient for understanding the whole containment phenomenon. Building an inductively analyzed holistic description and hypothesis of how containment works requires the identification and isolation, if possible, of many more variables. It is beyond the scope of this thesis to generate a statistical testing model capable of predicting whether a specific containment strategy is likely to enjoy success against a particular target. Qualitative research will however produce a military professional better capable of providing a policy maker with comprehensive advice on deterrent and containment topics.[3]

Qualitative research using case study methodology is appropriate for the post-Cold War section of this thesis because it is most useful to form or confirm theory, make comparisons, and offer generalized or transferable principles based on analytical results. Additionally, according to Paul Leedy and Jeanne Ormrod's research guide, case studies are ―especially suitable for learning more about a little known or poorly understood situation. It may also be useful for investigating how an individual or program changes over time, perhaps as the result of certain circumstances or interventions.‖[4] Before post-Cold War case studies can be scrutinized for similarities and differences to historical containment policies, a summary of those original policies must first be discussed. The thesis presents Cold War policies, as conceived and instituted by their respective presidential administrations, chronologically to establish the foundation which modern case studies can then be laid. This method aids understanding over time and assists the process of generating an initial hypothesis regarding containment's continued relevance.

Data Collection Overview

Chapter 2's literature review includes case studies and opinions written by historians, journalists, politicians, policy advisors, and professors of political science, history, law, and philosophy. The thesis author conducted no interviews, but thoroughly consulted multiple sources, including reviewing oral histories and declassified National Security Council documents from the Eisenhower Presidential Library at Abilene, Kansas to mitigate this limitation. Additional major sources include the resources of the Combined Arms Research Library at Fort Leavenworth, Kansas, online articles, and blogs. Conversations with Command and General Staff College (CGSC) professors additionally provided direction, guidance, and leads to other sources.

Specific data collection techniques for the three sections (containment policies; war and foreign policy theories; post-Cold War case studies) follow.

Data Collection: (1) Cold War Presidential Administration Containment Policies

A significant amount of historical content is required for adequate description of the most important containment events throughout the Cold War. This history serves as a building block and aids understanding of the follow-on post-Cold War applications. Though many competent historians have penned their accounts of the Cold War period, this thesis section relies heavily, though not exclusively, on the works of Dr. John Lewis Gaddis and personal recollections of primary policy makers. Gaddis, referred to by the *New York Times* as the ―Dean of Cold War historians,‖[5] is a widely respected multiple award-winning author and professor at Yale University, and remains well known for his seminal Cold War history and biographical books, most notably *Strategies of Containment*.[6] President George W. Bush awarded Gaddis the National Humanities Medal in 2005 for his contributions to understanding the linkages between diplomatic history and current events. The conscious decision to limit historical viewpoints avoids encumbrance in distracting debates over various historical accounts, while focusing the figurative spotlight on competing foreign policy theories, strategies, priorities, and degrees of effectiveness with containment application case studies. Furthermore, this limitation assists the evaluation methodology because it averts distorted analysis due to embedded biases multiple historians each include in their work, intended or otherwise. In other words, the Gaddis viewpoint (right or wrong) at least is consistent and therefore likely to produce more accurate analysis of differences with the containment policies of Cold War presidential administrations than an analysis of multiple historians' viewpoints.

Data Collection: (2) War and Foreign Policy Theories

Various theories of war and foreign policy influence a politician's mindset and decision-making process regarding containment. Unlike the choice to limit historical viewpoints for reasons stated above, the discussion of war theory and foreign policy decisions require consideration of multiple theorists. This thesis section therefore uses content analysis and qualitative analysis to judge which, if any, theories influenced Cold War policy makers. Resulting correlations compared with current policy makers will aid military professionals' understanding of their civilian bosses and assist them when dispensing advice in response to potential containment or deterrence situations.

<u>Data Collection: (3) Post-Cold War Case Studies</u>

Many post-Cold War case studies were available for analysis, including 1993's

―Dual Containment" policy[7] focused simultaneously on Iraq and Iran; evolving policies

toward Somalia from the 1990s to the present day; the Korean Peninsula; and current

policies toward Iran, China, Venezuela, and non-state terrorist organizations like al

Qaida. All of these case studies remain relevant and worthy of further study; however the

field was consciously narrowed for brevity purposes to one broad case study, and

extensive data collection was limited solely to it. The following briefly describes the

chosen U.S. foreign policy case study, and a concise justification for its inclusion

accompanies:

Somalia, 1993-Present. U.S. led multinational policy in Somalia, initiated by

President George Bush, and continued by President Clinton, began as a humanitarian

effort to ensure its people retained unfettered access to UN-supplied food shipments. Its

mission expanded to denying or containing warlord Mohamed Farrah Aidid's forces from

interfering with the original strictly humanitarian mission. The resulting debacle arguably

exists today as an example of reverse deterrence, in that U.S. lawmakers remain reluctant

to commit U.S. forces into Somalia to deal with its continuing chaos and rising threat.

Fifteen plus years of world neglect (African Union forces notwithstanding) toward

Somalia since its original withdrawal created the conditions pirates thrive on today. In

2009, Combined Task Force-151 (CTF-151) became a U.S. initiated, but multinationally-

led task force. According to its mission statement, CTF-151 specifically exists ―to

conduct counterpiracy operations under a mission-based mandate throughout the

Combined Maritime Forces (CMF) area of responsibility to actively deter, disrupt and

50

suppress piracy in order to protect global maritime security and secure freedom of navigation for the benefit of all nations."[8] The Somalia case study additionally presents the opportunity to evaluate containment's effectiveness or potential against non-state terrorist organizations because of Somalia's lack of governance capability. Organizations including al Shabaab, and the more commonly known al Qaida, present unique challenges due to its leaders and followers not being subjected to the international norms associated with statehood.

This case study analyzes U.S. policy toward under-governed countries like Somalia and non-state terrorist organizations through the Cold War containment lens in search of continued applicability.

Data Analysis

Analysis of the data began immediately upon commencement of collecting it. Merriam explains that analysis in a qualitative research project begins with the first read document and ―emerging insights, hunches, and tentative hypotheses direct the next phase of data collection, which in turn leads to the refinement or reformation of questions, and so on."[9]

The following steps of analytic induction are used:

1. Begin with tentative hypothesis explaining how containment works

2. Select a post Cold-War case study and see if it agrees with original hypothesis

3. Reformulate hypothesis if it does not fit; if it does fit, select additional case studies to continue testing

4. Consciously place apparently non-congruent case studies into hypothesis in an effort to bring all case studies into harmony with modified hypothesis

5. Hypothesis validated if no negative cases can be found.[10]

The analysis methodology presents tables to aid visualization of evaluation criteria and spot trends. These tables generate information useful for aiding understanding various foreign policies and forming initial hypotheses regarding whether a chosen foreign policy initiative enjoys success. Paragraphs detailing the analysis involved with decisions to plot each datum point accompany each table. The degree of policy success and its likely timetable to achieve it are beyond the scope of this thesis, as this requires a quantitative-like analytical approach. Follow-on research and analysis in this area are welcome.

<u>Verification of Standards</u>

An inherent flaw embedded with qualitative research is the fact that the primary instrument used throughout the process is human, and therefore subject to ―that human being‗s worldview, values, and perspective.‖[11] This limitation applies throughout the entire research process because the same person chooses the case studies, collects the data, analyzes it, and forms conclusions. Though the thesis captures other people‗s views, they still filter through the researcher‗s overall philosophy and understanding of how the world revolves.

Partial mitigation of this limitation relies on conscientious researcher effort, peer review, CGSC (ILE) faculty review, and to a somewhat lesser extent, triangulation of data sources.

Summary

This chapter succinctly describes the course of action for collecting and presenting salient information, analyzing what was gathered, and drawing defendable conclusions. It details the research methodology selected to answer the following main research question: How did the U.S. use of containment principles evolve during the Cold War, and does a correlation exist between those principles and today's foreign policies dealing with non-super power entities, including non-state actors such as terrorist organizations and their sponsor countries?

Answering the main question required breaking the data collection and analysis into three distinct sections, and each merited its own customized research method, but the thesis generally uses the qualitative case study method to generate chapter 4 analysis and follow-on conclusions in chapter 5. This method best facilitates the qualitative, logical analysis and presentation of findings because it identifies meaningful trends, patterns, or anomalies leading to generalized implications, thus fitting the thesis purpose of determining the level of containment theory's continued relevance.

---

[1]Sharan B. Merriam, *Qualitative Research and Case Study Applications in Education* (revised and expanded from Case Study Research in Education) (San Francisco, CA: Jossey-Bass, 1998), 4.

[2]Ibid., 6.

[3]Ibid., 9.

[4]Paul D. Leedy and Jeanne E. Ormrod, *Practical Research Planning and Design* 8th ed. (Upper Saddle River, NJ: Pearson Education, Inc., 2005), 139.

[5]Pricilla Johnson McMillan, "Cold Warmonger," *New York Times*, 25 May 1997, http://query.nytimes.com/gst/fullpage.html?res=9800EEDA1438F936A15756C0A96195 8260 (accessed 28 February 2011).

[6]John L. Gaddis, *Strategies of Containment* (New York, NY: Oxford University Press, 1982), ix.

[7]Laura Rosen, "Former NSC Aide on Clinton, 'Dual Containment', and HRC's 'Obliterate' Iran Remarks," *Mother Jones.com,* 8 May 2008, http://motherjones.com/mojo/2008/05/former-nsc-aide-clinton-dual-containment-and-hrcs-obliterate-iran-remarks (accessed 21 February 2011).

[8]Combined Task Force (CTF) 151, "Mission Statement," January 2009, http://www.cusnc.navy.mil/cmf/151/index.html (accessed 21 February 2011).

[9]Merriam, 151.

[10]Ibid., 160-61.

[11]Ibid., 22.

CHAPTER 4

ANALYSIS

Introduction

This chapter extracts and presents the analytical results of chapter 2's literature review in accordance with chapter 3's stated methodology. Similar to the previous chapters, this one is also divided into three sections, each of which deal with analyzing and answering the original question: How have U.S. containment policies changed throughout the Cold War, and do those policies contain relevancy to modern policy formulation, particularly toward non-state actors and terrorist organizations?

Analysis follows the same three-section subdivision pattern presented in earlier chapters:

Part 1: Cold War Containment Policies

Part 2: Theories of war and foreign policy as related to general deterrence and specific containment

Part 3: Post-Cold War non-state case studies

Part 1 Analysis

Cold War Presidential Administration's Containment Policies

Post WWII Policy Formation History and Truman Doctrine

The "Grand Alliance" countries responsible for defeating Nazism during WWII was doomed to unravel due to incompatible worldviews, though the invention and use of atomic weapons rapidly sped up the process. Stalin saw the A-bomb as "yet another challenge to his insistence that blood expended should equal influence gained: all at once, the U.S. had obtained a military capability that did not depend upon the deployment of armies on a battlefield. Brains—and the military technology they could produce—now counted for just as much."[1]

Stalin believed the U.S. would use the A-bomb as a way to gain favored concessions after the war at the expense of the USSR, and expressed his belief as ―A-bomb blackmail is American policy."[2] This belief, along with Stalin's direction to catch-up, helps explain the rapidity of the Grand Alliance's demise and the onset of the Cold War.

Roosevelt and Churchill discussed their post-war hopes, with their main goal being the elimination of the causes of war . . . at least their understanding of the causes of war. Their three main devices they planned in this endeavor included the following:

1. Cooperate among the great powers by salvaging components of Wilson's League of Nations and instituting its replacement, the United Nations. They intended this new organization to meet the collective security requirements for all participating nations.

2. Encourage political self-determination whenever possible.

3. Integrate each other's economic systems to encourage mutual trade.

Stalin's post-war strategy reflected virtually nothing in common with his current WWII allies. His vision was ―a settlement that would secure his own and his country's security while simultaneously encouraging the rivalries among capitalists that he believed would bring about a new war. Capitalist fratricide, in turn, would ensure the eventual Soviet domination of Europe"[3]

It is interesting to note that both the Soviets and the Capitalist West believed the seeds of self-destruction were each contained in each other's systems. Capitalist greed and its abuse of the working class, thought the Communists, would eventually create war among its practitioners, thus creating exploitable vulnerability. Likewise, free-market Capitalists believed Communism would eventually collapse from within due to its inherent weaknesses, including the tendency to strip away fundamental human freedoms and motivation to produce superior quality work output. Both beliefs were core to formulation of each country's Cold War policy.

George Kennan's Influence on Deterrence (Containment) Policy

The West watched as relations continued to deteriorate between themselves and their Grand Alliance partner in Moscow, but remained bereft of ideas or even a basic understanding of what to do about the matter. William Averell Harriman, the U.S. Ambassador in Moscow from 1943-1946 stated, "Unless we take issue with the present policy there is every indication [that] the Soviet Union will become a world bully whenever their interests are involved." He continued, "Gratitude cannot be banked with the Soviet Union."[4] President Truman subscribed to the philosophy that one can work with a totalitarian state, even one with a repugnant ideology, as long as they kept their word. The going-in argument was that the "quid pro quo" approach could actually work, though it was acknowledged that caution must be taken to avoid the appearance of appeasement, due to the liability that would create within Congress. The tactics included the appropriate use of sticks and carrots. The public shaming stick was deemed ineffective against a dictator like Stalin, and the ultimate nuclear stick would most likely never be used, so an alternate yet credible set of sticks needed to be found. Carrots, such as removing sanctions, extending economic aid, etc., needed to be linked to appropriate levels of concessions.

It is much more difficult to coordinate and deliver a precise package of deliverable carrots and sticks with a U.S. style democracy. There are a multitude of influences that must be dealt with and an impressive body of political waters to navigate. To list a few instances, deals occur among congressional committee members, various caucuses, White House officials, and even individual constituents. Dictatorships, such as what existed with Stalin's Soviet Union or modern North Korea, do not have these obstacles.

George F. Kennan, a highly respected but relatively junior Foreign Service Officer stationed at the American embassy in Moscow was given the task of assessing reasons why the Soviet Union behaved as it did, and why the Grand Alliance seemed doomed. Kennan's now famous, hastily written reply, came in the form of an 8,000-word cable, and was sent via telegram to Washington on 22 February 1946. "To say that it made an impact in Washington would be to put it mildly: Kennan's "long telegram" became the basis for U.S. strategy toward the Soviet Union throughout the rest of the Cold War."[5] Kennan's goal was to educate U.S. policy makers to better understand the situation they were facing when dealing with Soviet leaders. He felt that other countries' foreign policies were not always linked overtly as a reaction to what the West does, but was rather more likely tied to long-lasting internal issues. If Kennan could get U.S. policy makers to better understand those issues, there would be a much better chance successfully dealing with them through shaping their own countering policies.

Countries often need an enemy, whether it is a people, country, ideology, or otherwise. If at peace, those countries (the U.S. is not exempt) will often invent such an enemy to fill the gap. Part of deterrence strategy therefore can be to assist the direction of that ―need" to be filled by a more benign outlet such as global warming, or better yet, something we can all agree on such as counter-narcotics policy.

To summarize Kennan‘s post-WWII assessment of Moscow‘s basic nature:

1. Moscow‘s obstinacy was not driven by Western actions; rather the outside world was treated as hostile by Soviets because it provided the only excuse ―for the dictatorship without which they did not know how to rule, for cruelties they did not dare not to inflict, for sacrifices they felt bound to demand."

2. It is naïve to expect Western diplomatic concessions be reciprocated by Moscow.

3. Do not expect an alternate Moscow strategy until a future Kremlin leader (well beyond Stalin) realized enough policy failures and implemented a change.

4. War was not required (though it was possible) to achieve positive change in Moscow. Instead, Kennan articulated in an expanded version of his argument in 1947, a policy of ―long-term patient but firm and vigilant *containment* of Russian expansive tendencies" was needed.[6]

Kennan‘s newly found influence was tapped throughout the formation of Cold War policy. He advocated a policy of ―patience and firmness," and felt negotiators and leaders must show ―candor, courage, and self-confidence." His advice included the following:

1. Make disagreements open, but non-provocative

2. No concessions, but allow current possessions to stand

3. Increase military and extend economic and military aid to allies

4. Continue negotiating, but limit goals to gain acknowledgement of U.S. positions and acquire additional allies abroad

5. Project the image that the U.S. is –too strong to be beaten, and too determined to be frightened."[7]

Kennan's advocacy of –The Big Stick" was well known even though he greatly preferred the other instruments of national power. Speaking to students at the National War College in 1946, he said, –You have no idea, how much it contributes to the general politeness and pleasantness of diplomacy when you have a little quiet armed force in the background."[8] He believed that just having the military was probably the single most important factor of U.S. foreign policy. _Without the military's power, there is no credibility. Without credibility, there is no deterrence.' Kennan however did not believe a democracy could use its military as an offensive threat to anyone, and therefore should be a fixed, instead of mobile, factor of its foreign policy.

Military power can –only" be decisive when applied against a purely military problem. If the basic problem is political in nature, a military means will –not" achieve total victory. Temporary political acquiescence is achievable through military force, but politics, psychology, and especially economic policy, are the more likely and powerful tools to apply when trying to solve an essentially non-military or longer-term problem set.

Truman Doctrine and NSC-68

Kennan's counsel was evident throughout the Truman Doctrine, which was proclaimed on 12 March, 1947: "it must be the policy of the U.S. to support free peoples who are resisting attempted subjugation by armed minorities or outside pressures."[9] This statement, in effect, made the U.S. policy towards Greece and Turkey, who were helping the U.S. resist Soviet aims at expansion, applicable to the rest of the world. It is a good example of Kennan's "patience and firmness" policy. Interestingly though, as in most immediate postwar eras, drastic cuts were made in sustaining the huge capabilities of the military. This meant that even though the Truman Doctrine promised the world the "ends" that the U.S. would come to the aid of those resisting Soviet aggression, the "means" to accomplish those "ends" or goals were drastically being gutted due to budget cuts and military downsizing. This jeopardized the policy itself. No strategy can be expected to be taken seriously or have much of a probability to succeed if it does not have sufficient credibility (read military back-up power) to enforce it. Nuclear weaponry and its delivery mechanisms became the relied-upon stopgap in light of dwindling conventional power that would be required to address adequately the demands enforcing the Truman Doctrine entailed.

In contrast to the Truman Doctrine and NSC-68's claim of universal application (symmetrical containment), Kennan did not advocate equally helping everyone under threat of Communist expansion. Instead, he felt each situation needed evaluation on its own merits. Greece and Turkey (due to the bigger European picture) got the green light of approval, but China did not. Kennan's influence on the creation of the Marshall Plan reflected in the rationale for economically rehabilitating Western Europe: It would rebalance power, partially mitigate the problem of locally developing tendencies toward communism, and strain Moscow's influence in Eastern Europe. A case can be made that China is using these same postwar economic strategies against the U.S. today. China's economic development and assistance policies throughout the world, especially on the African continent, are buying influence while providing raw materials, and have the overall potential to marginalize U.S. global power.

Gaddis states that Kennan prophetically felt that ―direct military intervention to prevent communist takeover would only propel the U.S. into a series of civil wars from which it would be difficult to extricate itself.‖[10]

Countries experience differing levels of affluence and access to resources for a variety of reasons, including climate, education of its population, physical geography, and global events. A country enjoying relative wealth may chose to act globally in an expanded set of circumstances compared to that same country going through more challenging economic times. When inadequate monetary means exist, a nation is forced to differentiate between its vital interests and its peripheral interests. On other occasions, sufficient monies exist for substantive foreign policy to occur, yet priorities can be altered mainly due to the current leadership's personal convictions and persuasive abilities. Nobody argues against acting in accordance with the nation's vital interests. Debate arises when defining what is, or is not ―vital.‖ Something deemed as a national interest, but not vital, can, and often will, have action deferred or outright cancelled. It can be a fascinating spectator event to watch a country's internal debate regarding those two interests' fates. What may be ―vital‖ one day may find itself in the periphery the next.

Kennan stated in 1948 that the ―fundamental objectives of our foreign policy must always be

1. to protect the security of the nation, by which is meant the continued ability of this country to pursue the development of its internal life without serious interference, or threat of interference, from foreign powers; and

2. to advance the welfare of its people, by promoting a world order in which this nation can make the maximum contribution to the peaceful and orderly development of other nations and derive maximum benefit from their experiences and abilities.‖[11]

Kennan discussed two basic concepts relating to national security and dealing with the international community:

1. Universalism: This basic concept is ―Why can‗t we all just get along?‖ If all countries could somehow agree on a standard set of rules governing acceptable behavior, world order would be assured. This was attempted with President Wilson‗s League of Nations and later with the United Nations, but in order for it to be successful; the member nations would have to allow the international community to take care of everyone‗s security requirements. Problems arose upon realization that the League of Nations required significant individual sovereignty erosion, and the U.S. did not approve joining the League. The United Nations, shares similar sovereignty liabilities, and continues to struggle accordingly.

2. Particularized Approach: ―the thirst for power is still dominant among so many people that it cannot be assuaged or controlled by anything but counter-

63

force."[12] This concept does not have a problem with forming alliances, but it does postulate that these alliances must not be merely coalitions of short-term coinciding interests (i.e. USSR and allied western powers in WWII), but rather based on long-term common world views and goals. The alliances therefore must decidedly be limited in size.

Kennan's Give War a Chance?

Kennan was a pessimist about human nature, but a measured optimist when considering the U.S. capability for restraining international rivalries. ―The fact was that war might not always be evil; peace might not always be good: There is ‗peace' behind the walls of a prison, if you like that." ―People don't depart from the status quo peacefully when it is in their interest to maintain it."[13]

Containment Methods

Kennan proscribed a ―Containment by Exhaustion" method as a way to ensure U.S. national security. Its basic tenet was to identify the hostile and undependable entities in the world, and then work to encourage them to essentially fight it out amongst themselves, with the goal being to prevent any of them from turning those violent urges against the U.S. This was a ―bleed them to death" strategy, with the belligerents canceling each other out, thus leaving the rest of the world untouched. This method is rightly criticized as opposite from the principles the U.S. should stand for and morally repugnant, but though Kennan acknowledges principles themselves matter, he felt overall security mattered more. His rationale was that without security, one loses hope of applying principles (such as contributing to a better and more peaceful world). The U.S.

policy toward the Soviet Union's efforts in Afghanistan was an example of the containment by exhaustion strategy.

Another approach to containment uses diplomatic techniques, and wears the ―Containment by Integration" label. This method offers a belligerent country a prominent role in a postwar order. Western leaders attempted integration containment toward the Soviet Union following WWII, but succeeded mainly in creating an extremely powerful Soviet state, which lasted much longer than the brief alliance of WWII.

―Containment by Economic Policy" relies on a country creating sufficient dependence of a target country that it no longer poses a credible threat against it. Current U.S. dependency upon China to continue financing its deficit spending and accumulated debt could create sufficient deterrents that actual war is less likely to occur. One risk of such a conscious economic policy is that it could cause long-term resentment that will eventually spill over into violent actions intended to throw off the bonds of perceived servitude.

The U.S. did not have any tradition of limited war up to and including WWII, but with the advent of the nuclear age came the realization that a total war using these new weapons ―would be ‗suicidal' or at least ‗out of accord with every principle of humanity.'"[14] This prompted the U.S. to search for alternate means and policies to total war. The famous Charles Maurice de Tallyrand-Perigord quote furthers the point, ―nations ought to do one another in peace the most good, in war—the least possible evil."[15]

Containment Transferability

Kennan did not think or wish his containment strategy, devised for use against the Soviet Union, to be transferable and applied to other circumstances. He was extremely frustrated at the attempt to transfer containment to the Vietnam conflict. He angrily declared the sensation as having "inadvertently loosened a large bolder from the top of a cliff and now helplessly witness[ing] its path of destruction in the valley below, shuddering and wincing at each successive glimpse of disaster."[16]

While containment indeed was a disaster in Vietnam (though not necessarily the fault of containment principles), it was spectacularly successful over the long run against the Soviet Union. Gaddis explains and claims,

> "There was no war with the Soviet Union, as there had been twice with Germany and once with Japan between 1914 and 1945. There was no appeasement either, as there had been in the years between the two world wars. Whatever the oscillations between symmetry and asymmetry, whatever the miscalculations, whatever the costs, the U.S. and its allies sustained a strategy that was far more consistent, effective, and morally justifiable than anything their adversaries were able to manage. Indeed it is difficult to think of *any* peacetime grand strategy in which the results produced in the end correspond more closely with the objectives specified at the beginning."[17]

Kennan cautioned that containment policy had a more likely chance of success if applied in situations when there were no hard-fast timelines that the enemy is sticking to. He claimed that containment strategy would probably not have worked against Hitler or even Napoleon because they both were concerned with accomplishing their goals within their own lifetimes, thus prompting actions despite situations where caution would have been more prudent. Containment worked well against the Soviet Union because "the Kremlin is under no ideological compulsion to accomplish its purposes in a hurry."[18] He continued in his "X" article that, "Like the Church, it is dealing in ideological concepts which are of long-term validity. . . . It has no right to risk the existing achievements of the revolution for the sake of vain baubles of the future."[19]

Advancing this line of thought then, the question of applicability to today's threats must be asked. Can a containment strategy be successful against Somali pirates? Would a containment strategy against Iran be successful? How about against North Korea? Is Iran's revolution primarily motivated by long-term religious goals and principles, or does the current regime feel compelled to accomplish its stated goals within a condensed timeline? By what date does Pyongyang think it can achieve the reunification of the Korean Peninsula?

Eisenhower's New Look (―Massive Retaliation")

John Foster Dulles, President Eisenhower's Secretary of State, had been on record as opposing President Truman's containment policy even prior to the election. After becoming Secretary of State, he worked hard to convince Eisenhower that containment did not go far enough, and instead advocated a position that would ―roll back" the Soviets or ―liberate" countries that had fallen under Soviet control or domination. His opinions, expressed in his authorship of the Republican campaign's foreign policy platform during the Eisenhower campaign and several books and articles, shaped U.S. Cold War policy beyond the duration of his time in office, but were best remembered in his efforts to build up NATO as a component of Eisenhower's Massive Retaliation (New Look) policy.[20]

Eisenhower on 16 April 1953, gave The Chance for Peace speech (also referred to as the ―Cross of Iron" speech), but when the Soviets failed to respond, the newly elected President realized he needed to provide policy direction for his national security staff. Unsatisfied with the implementation and direction of Truman's containment policy, and wary of possible adverse consequences should his aggressive Secretary of State get his way undiluted, Eisenhower directed the formation of a special project to study three distinct courses of action to consider for his administration's foreign policy, especially concerning the Soviet and Communist expansion threat. Project Solarium, so-named due to the third floor location in the White House where it was discussed, became that special project.

Eisenhower chose two Army colleagues from his WWII experience, LTC Andrew J. Goodpaster and COL Robert R. Bowie, to lead two of the three task forces within Project Solarium.

Goodpaster, a West Point graduate and holder of a Ph.D. in international relations from Princeton, also happened to be the Army's leading expert on the role of nuclear weapons in war. He was currently serving as Eisenhower's Staff Secretary and Defense Liaison, and would eventually culminate his career as a four star general serving as NATO Supreme Commander.

Bowie held a Harvard law degree and served in the Army's legal division during the war. Afterward he directed the State Department's Policy Planning Staff and served as State's representative to the National Security Committee Planning Board. He later went on to become the Deputy Director of CIA for National Intelligence.

For the third course of action to be studied by Project Solarium (actually Task Force A) Eisenhower reached out to George F. Kennan, despite him being the chief architect of Truman's initial containment policy. Dulles himself had recently forced Kennan to leave the State Department due to differences of opinion as vocalized during the election campaign, but Eisenhower highly valued Kennan's intellect and thus offered

68

him the job. Kennan was surprised but flattered to be asked to serve, and was actually

disillusioned by Truman's implementation of his original containment theory, and

probably saw Solarium as a chance to correct the course.[21]

Kennan, leader of Task Force A, was charged with producing a policy that would

—modify, with additional initiatives, the Truman policy of containment."

Goodpaster, the nuclear weapons expert, led Task Force B, with its mission to

produce a policy that would —delineate the perimeters of U.S. security interests on the

globe and announce that should the Soviet Union or its allies cross those lines, war would

ensue."

Bowie, the State Department planner and legal expert, led Task Force C, whose

goal was to —propose measures short of war—including political, economic, diplomatic,

and covert—to eliminate Soviet influence from the free world and weaken communist

control in both Eastern Europe and in the Soviet Union itself."[22]

The Project Solarium exercise was carried out at the National War College, Fort

McNair in Washington D.C. from 10 June through 15 July, 1953 and used 21

participants, with seven in each task force. Kennan came away from the formal

presentation and recalled 35 years later that Eisenhower —spoke . . . with a mastery of the

subject matter and a thoughtfulness and a penetration that were quite remarkable. I came

away from it with a conviction (which I have carried to this day) that President

Eisenhower was a much more intelligent man than he was given credit for being."[23]

Among Solarium's findings were recommendations for —a U.S. capability for a

strong retaliatory offensive, a base for mobilization, and continental defense"; a —strong,

independent, and self-sufficient groupings of nations friendly to the U.S. centering on

Western Europe (including Germany), on the Far East (including Japan), and a position of strength in the Middle East."[24]

An oral history project captured the thoughts of Kennan, Goodpaster, and Bowie, 35 years after Project Solarium completed, and resulted with their following conclusions:

1. The USSR was a long-term vice imminent threat, and that threat would diminish if the U.S. acted wisely.

2. Conventional troop and weapons strength mattered, as did Soviet intimidation and alliances, but increasing nuclear weapons and delivery systems mattered more.

3. The U.S. needed to balance public alarm and complacency. The U.S. needed both conventional and nuclear systems and alliances to counterbalance the Soviet bloc.

4. Continue containment of Soviet power; do not ―roll back"; use allies.

5. Establish deterrent capacity and resolve; then use politics and education to ―convey the truth about capitalism, democracy, and human rights by various means to the populations of Eastern Europe and the Soviet Union."[25]

In addition to the above listed conclusions, Project Solarium enabled Eisenhower to brief his newly appointed NSC officials, establish his purposes and expectations, and build a crisis action plan if the need arose.

Eisenhower's adoption of a modified version of Truman's containment policy established the bi-partisan nature of U.S. foreign policy toward the Soviets. Granted, New Look moved away from NSC-68 and toward asymmetric containment, but the basic containment elements remained intact. This meant containment, as a national security strategy, enjoyed support from consecutive presidential administrations from differing

political parties. Containment was now neither Republican nor Democrat.

Kennedy and Flexible Response

Nuclear weapon capability continued to benefit from technological developments,

and their huge potential yields effectively made them too powerful to threaten their use

against anything but the absolute most aggressive actions from the Soviet Union. The

Kennedy Administration thus "attempted to institutionalize the notion of limited war,

including limited nuclear war, with a new doctrine: Flexible Response."[26] Instead of

promising an immediate and total nuclear response to any perceived Soviet aggressive

act, the U.S. and NATO would gradually escalate their responses in an effort to stop the

Soviets' operation. Flexible Response still reserved the right to use nuclear weapons if

the previously implemented escalatory steps failed, and it appeared the Soviet forces

were about to achieve victory. Despite these threats, all limited regional conflicts during

the Cold War were treated and fought as restricted conflicts, with much of the effort

devoted to ensuring nuclear escalation never occurred.[27]

Secretary of Defense, Robert McNamara, originally worked to provide the

President with more options during a possible nuclear war, and advocated plans calling

for strikes against Soviet forces instead of cities, "as a means of giving adversaries the

strongest imaginable incentive to refrain from striking our own cities."[28] He modified his

stance later though and, in a belief reminiscent to current National Defense Strategy, felt

that "deterring an attack (is) more important than limiting damage should one take

place."[29] This thinking took root, and "mutual assured destruction," also known by its

acronym MAD, sprouted roots as official policy by the end of Kennedy's Administration.

71

MAD, ―the idea that one's population could best be protected by leaving it vulnerable, so long as the other side faced comparable vulnerabilities," prompted the U.S. to proclaim a ―no first use" policy, while still clinging to reservations of first use under certain circumstances. Walt Rostow, a national security advisor to Kennedy wrote in 1962, ―We wish to assure them (USSR) that we do not intend to strike them first if they do not transgress the frontiers of the free community, but that we might well strike first under certain circumstances if they do."[30] This ambiguity and unpredictability worked as a deterrent virtue, and confirmed John Foster Dulles' earlier pronouncements stating unpredictability proved key to a successful deterrent policy.

Johnson (Flexible Response Continued)

Lyndon Johnson's unexpected route to assuming the presidency and similar ideologies preserved much of Kennedy's Flexible Response stance toward containment strategy. Both leaders shared a ―zero-sum game" worldview, as did the Eisenhower Administration, in that any Communist victory must be seen as a loss for the U.S. ―Kennedy commented two months before his death, _that every time a country, regardless of how far away it may be from our own borders . . . passes behind the Iron Curtain the security of the U.S. is thereby endangered.'"[31] Johnson followed suit after Kennedy's assassination the following year with the statement that ―surrender anywhere threatens defeat everywhere."[32] These statements firmly swung the containment pendulum back into the symmetrical camp, and resulted in a NSC-68-like policy ―in its commitment to flexible but appropriate response regardless of cost; different from that earlier document, though, in its vagueness regarding just what was to be contained."[33]

72

Nixon's Détente

Richard Nixon's enduring reputation as a staunch ideologically rigid anti-Communist gave him a unique advantage over political rivals not possessing his credentials. Instead of being perceived as soft against Communists when negotiating, he achieved an ―aura of statesmanship . . . thus according him greater freedom of action than his more liberal rivals for the presidency could have expected."[34] Nixon's choice as national security advisor was Dr. Henry Kissinger, who strongly pulled the nation back onto an asymmetrical containment path, albeit in significantly new ways.

―What this odd alliance of Nixon and Kissinger sought was a strategy that would combine the tactical flexibility of the Kennedy-Johnson system with the structure and coherence of Eisenhower's, while avoiding the short-sighted fixations that had led to Vietnam or the ideological rigidities of a John Foster Dulles."[35] Gaddis writes that the ―Nixon-Kissinger strategy returned, in its underlying assumptions, to many of the ideas on which George Kennan had based his original strategy of containment more than two decades before. Containment, it seemed, was coming back to concerns and concepts that had animated it during the earliest days of the Cold War—and those ideas were being used, as Kennan had hoped to use them, to try to end the Cold War."[36] Indeed, Kennan said a year after Kissinger was appointed Secretary of State that ―Henry understands my views better than anyone at State ever has."[37]

Kissinger felt it was simplistic to believe that power was a ―zero sum game." Rather than insist that a loss for the U.S., like the stalemate in Vietnam, was an automatic win for the Soviet Union, a corresponding and compensating opening to China could offset this loss. ―It was the overall calculus of power that was important, not the defeats or victories that might take place in isolated theaters of competition." Nixon and Kissinger insisted on demonstrating that America's power and commitment throughout the world should not be symbolized by its performance in Vietnam, but by its overall global relationships.[38]

Strategic changes implemented under the Nixon-Kissinger watch included injecting a realism mentality, and a cessation of effort to impose American-style democracy on other societies. Kissinger, expressing this line of thought said, ―What was needed, was the realism to accept the world as it was, together with the ingenuity to make the best of it."[39] Another major shift in strategic thinking saw defense policy change from maintaining superiority across the board to one that was merely sufficient to ensure effective deterrence of the Soviet Union. Ever cautious that a sufficiency policy would be perceived as exploitable weakness by the Soviet Union, Kissinger and Nixon made it a point to emphasize that seeking or obtaining superior strength led to increased tension and war. Nixon elaborated in a 1972 *Time* magazine article that, ―The only time in the history of the world that we have had any extended period of peace is when there has been a balance of power. It is when one nation becomes infinitely more powerful in relation to its potential competitor that the danger of war arises. . . . I think it will be a safer world and a better world if we have a stronger, healthy U.S., Europe, Soviet Union, China, Japan, each balancing the other, not playing one against the other, an even balance."[40]

The Nixon-Kissinger team took full advantage of the growing Sino-Soviet schism while cultivating this new five-power global balancing act. Gaddis explains that ―in an age of shared nuclear peril, even the most ideologically antagonistic states could find interests in common."[41]

New relationships with Communist China, determination not to be totally humiliated by the situation in Vietnam, and the perceived need to continue to take stands against communist expansion drove the administration into adopting the strategy known as détente. Though no word in English or Russian captured its meaning accurately, Gaddis says the Nixon-Kissinger team clearly viewed détente as, ―yet another in a long series of attempts to _contain' the power and influence of the U.S.S.R., but one based on a new combination of pressures and inducements that would, if successful, convince Kremlin leaders that it was in their country's best interest to be _contained'."[42]

Ford (Détente Continued)

President Ford's retention of Henry Kissinger as his powerful Secretary of State ensured the continuity of the détente foreign policy throughout his short tenure.[43] This did not mean Ford refrained totally from delving into smaller examples of Communist expansionism such as Angola, even though no evidence directly linked that country's Marxist independence movement to Kremlin involvement.[44] Tolerance of communism, at least to the point of détente, among countries that significantly mattered geopolitically, like China and the Soviet Union while maintaining a hard line against Angola and Chile were indeed contradictory. Realist policy makers believed Communist expansion could be successfully resisted in some Third World countries (Vietnam notwithstanding), but recognized when tacit cooperation was required from the larger countries like China.

Carter Doctrine

President Carter had extreme difficulty constructing a coherent foreign policy to continue effectively containing the Soviet threat. He entered office somewhat downplaying the belief —that Soviet expansion was almost inevitable."[45] Carter continued, —It is a new world that calls for a new American foreign policy—a policy based on common decency in its values and on optimism in our historical vision."[46] The later Soviet invasion of Afghanistan prompted him to drastically and immediately alter course. He increased defense spending, considered reconstituting the military draft, and issued statements like making the Soviets —pay a concrete price for their aggression." His self-proclaimed Carter Doctrine warned the Kremlin that —any attempt by any outside force to gain control of the Persian Gulf region will be regarded as an assault on the vital interests of the U.S., and such an assault will be repelled by any means necessary, including military force."[47]

Gaddis points out that Carter's almost desperate attempt to create a distinct foreign policy pushed him away from both the symmetrical and asymmetrical schools of thought. Carter emphasized human rights and morality, which shared typical Democratic symmetrical platforms. He leaned in the asymmetrical direction however, by largely keeping substantive Kissinger policies intact. He —retained the Republicans' asymmetrical approach of differentiating between vital and peripheral interests, of distinguishing between levels of threat, and of keeping responses commensurate with means. He continued Kissinger's practice of working with some Communists to contain others."[48] Carter unwittingly pursued contradictory policies in an attempt to —win the support of critics on the Right who had objected to Kissinger's _appeasement' of the

76

Soviet Union, and those on the Left who had worried about his _amorality.'"[49] This

confusion, coupled with Carter's own advisors, Brzezinski as National Security Advisor

and Vance as Secretary of State, disagreeing about priorities effectively doomed any

chances for real success with Moscow.

Reagan's Peace Through Strength

President Reagan came into office determined to deal with the Brezhnev Doctrine,

—to intervene whenever _external and internal forces hostile to socialism try to turn the

development of a given socialist country in the direction of the restoration of the

capitalist system.'"[50] Reagan's belief, according to Gaddis: —His rejection of Mutual

Assured Destruction, and hence of the Strategic Arms Limitation Talks (SALT) process,

stemmed from a long-standing conviction that relying on nuclear weapons to keep the

peace was certain sooner or later to bring on a nuclear war. Détente itself, he believed,

had frozen the nuclear age in place, rather than doing anything to alleviate it."[51] This

belief moved Reagan to start pushing for a policy that would therefore move from the

previous SALT to one that would actually result in a reduction of nuclear weapons:

START (Strategic Arms Reduction Talks).

The Strategic Defense Initiative (SDI), commonly known at the time as —Star

Wars" was —a striking demonstration of killing multiple birds with a single stone: in one

speech Reagan managed simultaneously to pre-empt the nuclear freeze movement, to

raise the prospect of not just reducing but eliminating the need for nuclear weapons, to

reassert American technological preeminence, and, by challenging the Soviet Union in an

arena in which it had no hope of being able to compete, to create the strongest possible

incentive for Soviet leaders to reconsider the reasons for competition in the first place."[52]

Reagan went radically further when he even offered to share SDI technology with the Soviets as a demonstration of his sincerity of reducing the threats of nuclear missiles.

Though the Carter Administration did challenge the Soviet system on their human rights record, the Reagan Administration was the first American presidency to frame its Soviet containment strategy in a way that would deliberately target the Kremlin's leadership by exploiting their economic weaknesses, tensions with satellite states, and socialist doctrine itself. Reagan's first national strategy directive in May 1982 explicitly called for ―efforts to force _the USSR to bear the brunt of its economic shortcomings, and to encourage long-term liberalizing and nationalist tendencies within the Soviet Union and allied countries.‘"[53]

The three main points Reagan wished to convey to the Soviets (Gorbachev):

1. ―The United States was sincere in seeking to lower the danger of nuclear war."[54]

2. ―A command economy, when coupled with authoritarian politics, was a prescription for obsolescence in the modern world." Reagan's famous line regarding this thinking came from a speech in May 1981: ―The West won't contain communism, it will transcend communism. It won't bother to . . . denounce it, it will dismiss it as some bizarre chapter in human history whose last pages are even now being written."[55]

3. ―The Soviet Union had itself become, over the years, what it had originally sought to overthrow—an oppressive empire."[56]

This last point, otherwise known today as the Reagan Doctrine, was ―A plan to turn the forces of nationalism against the gains the Soviet Union had made in recent years in the _third world', and eventually against its sphere of influence in Eastern Europe itself."[57]

Secretary of State George Shultz believed that reducing overall capabilities for both the U.S. and the Soviet Union made sense because he, like President Reagan, believed the Soviets were so far behind the U.S. and its allies in virtually every other aspect. He told his staff in 1986 that, ─The Soviet Union is a superpower only because it is a nuclear and ballistic missile superpower."[58]

As mentioned previously within his own quote, Reagan moved beyond mere containment of communism. His strategy however still fit within broad containment theory. Reagan assumed unlimited resources, meaning that he thought the U.S. could and would always be able to outspend the Soviet Union. This therefore biased his strategy to the symmetrical side of the containment theories. ─In contrast to the authors of NSC-68 and the strategists of the Kennedy and Johnson administrations, however, Reagan made this calculation on the basis of what the Soviet economy, not his own, could withstand."[59] This difference pointed toward an asymmetric camp strength, in that it set the conditions to favor the U.S. strengths. However, because he did not respond equally to every perceived Soviet act of aggression, he did not fall into the same traps that asymmetrical advocates became victims of during the Korean and Vietnam experiences. He never wavered diplomatically however in giving moral support to those areas in need. He thus ─insulated his administration from the fears of falling dominoes and the moral qualms that had beset practitioners of asymmetrical containment."[60] Reagan's overall policy, since it incorporated both sides' strengths, while avoiding their weaknesses, created a different strategy than containment. His was more a policy of ─changing" rather than

―containing" the adversary. Henry Kissinger praised the administration: ―Reagan's was an astonishing performance, and to academic observers, nearly incomprehensible. . . . When all was said and done, a president with the shallowest academic background was to develop a foreign policy of extraordinary consistency and relevance."[61]

Cold War Containment Analysis

Table 1 summarizes key aspects, conditions, and philosophies of presidential administrations from Truman to Reagan. First, Cold War Democratic presidents consistently subscribed to the symmetrical containment philosophy, though Carter's confused foreign policy did show signs of siding with the asymmetrical camp on occasion. Democrats' strong sense of moral duty to strongly, and militarily oppose Communism, regardless of location and immediate threat to the U.S., explains the symmetrical mindset tendency.

Democratic presidents, who felt obligated to fight symmetrically against perceived Communist expansive tendencies, committed to both the Cold War's two major conflicts, Korea and Vietnam. Granted, Republican legislators approved and provided financing for these actions, but it remains clear that symmetrical philosophies led the call to arms for both Korea and Vietnam.

Economic hard times, including post WWII downturns and economic recessions occurred under both Republican and Democratic presidential administrations. While an asymmetric containment policy inherently costs less to implement, mainly because it does not obligate large conventional military responses globally, the analysis does not conclusively link the country's economic condition to which containment variant dominated. Indeed, the economic boom during the Reagan Administration still saw symmetrical containment policy, whereas Nixon's mostly positive economic climate experienced asymmetrical containment.

President Reagan's Administration showed the most anomalies. His was the only Republican administration to favor symmetrical containment, though the President did convert over to the Republican Party from the Democrats prior to his election as California Governor. While not committing U.S. troops in large numbers or for long periods against Communist countries, his willingness to use force against its spread in Grenada and his support of the Contras in Nicaragua clearly illustrated his symmetrical tendencies. Unlike any other Cold War President, Reagan uniquely chose to focus his containment strategy on taking advantage of Soviet weaknesses, rather than countering their strengths. Insufficient data exists to determine whether adopting a weakness-centric strategy is superior to a countering strengths strategy however, as Reagan's is the only example, and the Soviet Union's economy had been declining prior to his administration.

Containment, as a strategy, is inherently defensive in nature, hence the majority of presidents defaulting their policies toward defending against the Soviet Union's military might. This makes Reagan's choice to choose a more offensive minded strategy all the more extraordinary, since he targeted the Kremlin's weaknesses instead. No conclusive evidence exists that this policy characteristic is solely responsible for the Soviet Union's demise, but it certainly was a contributing factor. For this reason, it behooves the modern containment or deterrence planner to consider a strategy that uses offensive components, as well as the traditional defensive elements that merely keep the targeted entity or phenomenon from gaining territory or influence.

Table 1.   Cold War Containment Analysis

	Conflict committing large # of US troops?	Recession or economic constraints?	Symmetrical Containment?	Asymmetrical Containment?	Policy Focus: Soviet Strength or Weakness?
Truman	Y (Korea)	Y	Y	N	Strength
Eisenhower	N (Armistice)	Y	N	Y	Strength
Kennedy	N	N	Y	N	Strength
Johnson	Y (Vietnam)	N	Y	N	Strength
Nixon	Y (Vietnam)	N	N	Y (Détente)	Strength
Ford	N	Y	N	Y (Détente)	Strength
Carter	N	Y	Y	Y	Strength
Reagan	N	N	Y	N	Weakness

Source: Created by author.

Part 2

Theory: War, Foreign Policy, Deterrence, and Containment

Before delving deeply into deterrence and containment theory, it is critical to take a step back and analyze different worldviews in order to understand why politicians adopt or reject different foreign policies. These disparate foreign policies necessarily result in variances in formulation and implementation of deterrence policies and containment strategies, as might be expected.

The chapter 2 literature review includes works from historians and theorists specializing in containment strategy, deterrence theory, and the nature of conflict, as well as fairly wide ranging thoughts from political scientists, professors, and respected opinion makers including documentary film producers, journalists, lawyers and military personnel. This chapter section analyzes various theories, and displays resulting distillates as characteristics of presidential administrations from Truman to Reagan.

There are limits of foreign policy theory, due in large part to the fact that theories simplify reality. Cold War foreign policy maker and principle author of NSC-68, Paul Nitze, criticized theorists and their works when he stated that "Most of what has been written and taught under the heading of political science' by Americans since WWII has been . . . of limited value, if not counterproductive, as a guide to the actual conduct of policy."[62]

While the lament is understandable, it is also important to understand that foreign policy theory is essential for policy makers because they must have a framework or starting point of understanding as to how they believe the world really works. There is no sense in devising and implementing random, disconnected bits of policy that do not have an intended fused result. Politicians will more likely than not choose a theorist that conforms closely to his or her ideology, and then create a foreign policy that fits within the selected theory's parameters. The caution however, is that because theories are simplifying, they must ignore certain variables and factors, while emphasizing the perceived main or causal factors for a given situation of condition. This explains why any given theory cannot always account for every observed phenomenon in reality.

Offensive and Defensive Realism Theories

Mearsheimer's theory, Offensive Realism, states that anarchy and the distribution of power are the factors that matter most for explaining international politics, and therefore used as predictors of a country or non-state actor's future behavior.[63] A country will naturally gravitate toward achieving regional dominance, and once achieved, will seek ways to prevent any other players from gaining power that could interfere with its hegemony. This tendency explains why Mearsheimer rejects the common claim that democracies do not fight each other. He feels that even if a country's political system uses democratic ideals, it will still naturally attempt to become a regional hegemony, and will work to ensure possible competition in its area of influence is minimized.[64] He admits that his theory largely ignores factors such as personalities (who is in power at any given time) and ideology. Extrapolating from this Offensive Realism theory then, formulating an effective containment policy must account for the targeted country's tendency to acquire dominant status, and tactics must be devised to counteract, dilute, or neutralize those efforts.

Mearsheimer's Offensive Realism theory is opposed by those subscribing to its opposite, Defensive Realism, including Kenneth Waltz and Charles Glaser. Defensive Realism theorists believe it is possible for countries to achieve adequate security, whether by creating a viable second-strike nuclear capability or otherwise. Other differences between Offensive and Defensive Realism theories includes the latter's belief that domestic politics and individual states' communication of intentions can avert hostilities.[65]

Liberal Foreign Policy Theories

The following three leading liberal foreign policy theories, according to Mearsheimer, are responsible for driving much of deterrence strategy formulation, though his Offensive Realism argument counters them:

The claim[s] that

1. Prosperous and economically interdependent states are unlikely to fight each other.
2. Democracies do not fight each other.

84

3. International institutions enable states to avoid war and concentrate instead on building cooperative relationships.[66]

At the risk of sounding like a circular argument, if the above listed theories' tenets contain perceived truth regardless of Mearshimer's skepticism, it follows that an Administration not seeking geographical expansion would institute policies and conditions that bolster the odds of achieving those same tenets' contents. For instance, a country can set its economic policy in a way that encourages international investment and financing, thus setting a course aimed at creating ~~p~~rosperous and economically interdependent states." Evidence of this policy is clearly visible between the U.S. and China today. While the military threat these countries pose toward each other is inarguably growing at a rapid pace, the fact that they are economically dependent upon each other may actually prove to be the key to keeping the great powers from unleashing their militaries' might against each other. Is this deterrence however? Perhaps not in the traditional sense, which would require the credible threat of undesirable consequence should an undesirable action be taken. However, keeping the same U.S. and China example, the undesirable consequence for China, should they decide to exercise its military capability against the U.S., would include the forfeiting of its sizable credit balance it currently enjoys. The argument continues that China simply cannot afford to militarily attack U.S. interests due to fear of non-repayment of outstanding loans. Though traditional fear of U.S. military response would certainly compound Beijing's calculus with said scenario, the economic deterrence component arguably holds greater sway.

Just War Theory

Michael Walzer states that, "war is sometimes justifiable and that the conduct of war is always subject to moral criticism."[67] This statement satisfies neither the pacifist, nor the realist because pacifists never believe war can ever be justifiable, and realists believe that laws are not applicable during war (all's fair in love and war). It is this perceived middle ground that gives "Just War" theory its broad appeal to most U.S. policy makers, and thus shapes their follow-on formulation of deterrence policy.

The following are two common criticisms of "Just War" theory along with Walzer's paraphrased responses:

1. Those who defend and apply the theory of just war merely make it easier to moralize war and therefore make it easier to fight.

   Response: While war is always terrible and keeping in mind that it is the business of killing, sometimes it still is the moral (therefore just) response to a situation. Walzer cites Nazism in WWII as a justifiable war and the Rwanda genocide in 1994 as an example of a situation that met Just War criteria, but was not acted on.[68]

2. It frames the war the wrong way. Specifically it focuses the debate on the issues before war commences such as, in Iraq's case prior to Operation Iraqi Freedom, on inspections, disarmament, WMD, etc. It thus neglects to consider adequately the broader questions pointing to broader motivations including imperialism, global resources, and power.

   Response: There is no rule limiting the scope of criticism when analyzing the *justness* of a particular war. While the immediate run-up to a war may get the

86

lion's share of public scrutiny due to the simple fact of its proximity, there is

no reason why the debate cannot expand to include its overall actual (or

perceived) motivations.[69]

Walzer states, ―Aggressive wars, wars of conquest, wars to extend spheres of

influence and establish satellite states, wars for economic aggrandizement—all these are

unjust wars.‖[70] The unanswered question then regarding Walzer's previous assertion is

what happens if there is a collateral effect from an otherwise just war that includes one or

more of the unjust characterizations he listed? Can a war against Iraq, in which the U.S.

has no long-term intent to occupy or establish as a satellite state, but does have the hope

of influencing (or at least providing a counterbalance to Iran) as well as create a more

stable oil-exporting region, still be justifiable?

Horrific examples of worldwide massacres and ethnic cleansing episodes in

Bosnia, Kosovo, Rwanda, the Sudan, Sierra Leone, the Congo, Liberia, and East Timor

led Walzer to call for the expansion of Just War theory from the standard two, to the

following three components:

> 1. Jus ad bellum (decision to go to war)
> 2. Jus in bello (conduct of the battles)
> 3. Jus post bellum (justice after the war) *
> * recommended because it will expand the Just War debate to include nation
> building, establishment of protectorates, and long-term military occupations.[71]

The Moral Component of Just War Theory

―In a war for hearts and minds, rather than for land and resources, justice turns out

to be the key to victory.‖[72] Can acting in the interests of a nation or the nation's people be

considered a moral act? If so, is it still moral if that act causes harm to the targeted nation,

its people, or organization?[73] While pondering these questions, consider Walzer's

87

definition of national interest: ―The objectively determined sum of power and wealth here and now plus the probability of future power and wealth."[74] If this definition is accepted, then should an elected leader of a democratic republic, such as the U.S., always act in the national interest? Are there moral limits of national interest? Elected politicians each carry their own moral character into office, and their foreign policies each reflect that character. Regardless however, all U.S. Presidents from the Cold War to present day continue to explain their foreign policy intervention and containment policies with deference and consideration of Just War theory.

Morality has a tendency to warp depending on how dire the surrounding circumstances are. War situations sometimes use utilitarian calculation. Walzer lists the justification progression of a specific segment of a population being deliberately targeted to the attacking country's constituents, with later list entries increasingly controversial:

1. Enemy soldiers actually engaged in combat
2. Enemy soldiers not actually engaged in combat at the time they are attacked
3. Civilians employed by war-related industries
4. Civilians who support the war indirectly
5. Everyone else who supports the supporters, the workers, and the soldiers
6. Infants of the enemy, because even their deaths will help undermine the enemy's resolve.[75]

This process led to the justification during WWII for the bombing campaigns against civilian populated areas by the British during their Churchill-declared time of ―supreme emergency." Whereas normal, or at least less stressful times, would impose stricter moral limits, extreme times where a nation's very existence is at stake, utilitarianism and its accompanying rationalism will allow acts of war that would never be tolerated in a lesser situation. Morality itself is either suspended or drastically modified to allow what some would consider an evil. Can the premeditated killing of civilians be more moral than allowing one's own country's citizens to be captured by the enemy? Churchill's Great Britain faced that predicament, and factored heavily when making the conscious decision to bomb civilian-occupied areas of Germany. President Truman's decision to use a nuclear bomb against Hiroshima was justified to the American people by promising them that it would end the war sooner and therefore save more American troops' lives. The fact that it indiscriminately killed thousands of Japanese civilians was insufficient to dissuade the decision to use the bomb.

Deterrence is most often considered when trying to keep an entity from carrying out an undesired action. In a way however, the U.S. nuclear bombing of Japan can be considered a form of —lethal deterrence," albeit in an ultimate manner. The U.S. was obviously already in a war with Japan, and therefore was not trying to deter Tokyo from attacking in the first place. Refer back to JP 5-0's definition of deterrence: —The prevention from action by fear of the consequences. Deterrence is a state of mind brought about by the existence of a credible threat of unacceptable counteraction."[76] U.S. nuclear actions were congruent with this definition, in that they brutally demonstrated both credibility and capability, and were designed to prevent Japan from deciding to continue the war. A less dramatic example of lethal deterrence exists with NATO's current —No-Fly Zone" operations in Libya. In Libya's case, a state of war exists between Muammar Qaddafi's loyal forces and those rebelling to his continued authority. NATO's operation attempts to deter Qaddafi from using his aircraft (and now ground units) against the rebels by lethally engaging his forces. Lethal deterrence, as a recognized variation of policy, remains undeveloped, possibly for morality reasons.

89

So, if an argument can be made for a country that, in the case of ¬supreme

emergency," morality can be suspended, what is to prevent an individual soldier from

exercising that same right when his life is at stake?[77] Walzer's example is the case of

when killing prisoners is safer for the soldier than taking the extra risks of transporting

them to a holding facility. The reason for the perceived double standard is that an

individual is expected to assume personal risk, but a government representative should

not be assuming unlimited risk for his/her citizens. They have more of an obligation to

protect the greater population than to impose collective risk for morality's sake.[78] Marcus

Luttrell's harrowing personal account of his experience in Afghanistan in his book *Lone*

Survivor describes the agonizing decision to let three stumbled upon goatherds go with

the full knowledge that his Sea Air and Land (SEAL) team would likely be compromised

and exposed to more danger from pursuing Taliban. Morality and fear of probable

criminal charges dominated their discussion, and to this day, Luttrell believes their

decision was a mistake.[79] A political leader whose philosophy does not allow

distinguishing between individual versus collective governmental responsibility risks

national security.

¬A morally strong leader is someone who understands why it is wrong to kill the

innocent and refuses to do so, refuses again and again, until the heavens are about to fall.

And then he becomes a moral criminal (like Albert Camus's ̠just assassin') who knows

that he can't do what he has to do—and finally does."[80]

When is it acceptable for a country to get their hands dirty? While Walzer defends

the British bombing in 1940 and 1941 against German cities, he does not believe it was

right to do once it became clear that Germany would lose. Once the imminent danger to

Britain was past, the normal obligation to protect innocent citizens (even those of enemy nations) goes back into effect.[81] Had the continued bombing campaign been designed from the outset as a deterrent against the continued Nazi war against Jews (which it never was), there might have been some justification.

Paradoxically, a true "supreme emergency" morally requires a nation to act immorally. The Cold War used an extended long-term stance on "supreme emergency" in that the U.S. felt compelled to immorally threaten the Soviet Union with nuclear destruction due to the countering threat that the Soviet Union posed back on the U.S.

Because a country's containment strategy involves an inherent risk of sparking an actual war, carefully consider Just War theory before applying an actual containment policy against a targeted country. The old saying of "Don't point a weapon at anything you don't want to shoot" is applicable on a grander strategic scale as well. Walzer elaborates:

> I suggested in *Just and Unjust Wars* that nuclear deterrence was commonly defended, and rightly defended, in terms that follow closely the lines of the supreme-emergency argument. Were terror unbalanced—so both sides believed—country and culture, people and way of life, would alike be at risk. And so we permitted ourselves to threaten the same terrorism that we feared: the total destruction of cities, the killing of vast numbers of innocent men, women, and children. The threat was immoral, for it is wrong to threaten to do what it would be wrong to do; and though the threat is obviously a lesser wrong than the act, it can hardly be taken lightly when it is accompanied by massive preparation for the act.
>
> We accepted the risk of nuclear war in order to avoid the risk, not of ordinary, but of totalitarian, subjugation. If that second risk were to recede (as it has), we would be bound to seek alternatives to deterrence in its cold-war form. In any case, we are bound to look for ways of reducing the risk—by pursuing détente, for example, or by signing arms-control and arms-reduction agreements, or by undertaking unilateral initiatives that address the fears and suspicions of the other side. We must resist the routinization of emergency, reminding ourselves again and again that the threats we force others to live with, and live with ourselves, are immoral threats. Over the years we became habituated, callous, hardened against

91

the crimes we were pledged to commit. But it isn't incompatible with the pledges to think concretely about those crimes and about our own unwilling criminality—for it won't be unwilling unless we think about it. This is the essential feature of emergency ethics: that we recognize at the same time the evil we oppose and the evil we do, and that we set ourselves, so far as possible, against both.[82]

Preemption vs. Prevention

There are real differences between the concepts of preemption and prevention. The official National Security Strategy (December 2002) used the two words interchangeably, thus leading much of the controversy today. This document, which came to be known as the "Bush Doctrine" was the first time that preemption (or more accurately prevention) was openly published as a central tenet of U.S. National Security Policy. Preemption is not now, nor really ever was controversial. Preemption is usually considered outside the realm of containment because it involves taking action against an attack either already in progress or extremely imminent. Prevention, on the other hand, if articulated as official policy, could find shelter under containment's umbrella.

> Dr. Colin S. Gray writes, as seen in chapter 1's definitions, that to
>
> preempt means to strike first (or attempt to do so) in the face of an attack that is either already underway or is very credibly imminent. The decision for war has been taken by the enemy. The victim or target state can try to disrupt the unfolding assault, or may elect to receive the attack before reacting." Prevention, on the other hand –is a war of discretion. It differs from preemptive war both in its timing and in its motivation. The preemptor has no choice other than to strike back rapidly; it will probably be too late even to surrender. The preventor, however, chooses to wage war, at least to launch military action, because of its fears for the future should it fail to act now.[83]

Alan Dershowitz, the Harvard Law School professor and pro-Israeli lobbyist, pointed out in his book *Preemption: A Knife that Cuts Both Ways* that if prevention were successfully executed, neither the preventer nor the rest of the world would ever know the extent of what exactly was prevented. A major problem with prevention theory (as well as preemption and deterrence): If successfully executed, the preventer (and often the

world at large) will never know the extent of what exactly was prevented. Dershowitz

uses the example of WWII:

> Had the United States (or Great Britain) attacked German military targets in the
> 1930s, *before* Germany's aggression against Poland, and had it prevented the
> German conquest of Europe with its enormous casualties, the historical
> assessment of preventive war might well have been quite different. Indeed, it is
> the inaction of Chamberlain that has become a paradigm of immoral and
> ineffective appeasement. But if Hitler's Germany had been destroyed or disarmed
> by preventive military action, the world would have experienced only British
> ―aggression," which, despite Germany's violation of its treaty obligations, might
> have seemed disproportionately harsh without actual knowledge of what might
> have been. This is the paradox of prevention: When it is employed successfully,
> we rarely can be sure of what it prevented. When it is not employed, it is difficult
> to assess if it could actually have prevented the horrors that did occur.[84]

Professor Robert Pape's (author of *Dying to Win*) political ideology is

demonstrated with his comment: ―Preventive war by the U.S. would violate one of the

most important norms of international politics—that democracies do not fight preventive

wars." Just because Pape's statement (made prior to the U.S. invasion of Iraq) reflected

accurate history, it does not follow that the U.S. should ―never" fight a preventive war.

As the example of WWII shows, an argument can easily be made that the U.S. ―should"

have fought a preventive war, despite the Pape-cited ―norms of international politics."[85]

Princeton professor Richard Falk criticized the Iraq preventive efforts as flimsily

justified,

> on the basis of shadowy intentions, alleged potential links to terrorist groups,
> supposed plans and projects to acquire weapons of mass destruction, and
> anticipations of possible future dangers. It is a doctrine without limits, without
> accountability to the U.N. or international law, without any dependence on a
> collective judgment of responsible governments and, what is worse, without any
> convincing demonstration of practical necessity.[86]

Professor Falk seems to believe that demonstrating legitimacy and conforming to the expectations and tolerances of the international norms trumps the perceived national security and sovereignty of the U.S.

Preventive Action Justification

Two commonly used justifications for preventive action include:

1. Rogue states and terrorists increasingly have access to means of attack that would result in massive casualties and economic damage, and therefore cannot be allowed to strike if there is any prevention option.

2. The U.S. has superior information/intelligence gathering and analysis capability, as well as vastly improved strategic strike capabilities. This capability, if not used when actionable intelligence is in hand, would be immoral.[87]

A 1997 National Security Program report from Harvard's Kennedy School listed five key intelligence components that must be analyzed and fused into a cohesive picture for decision makers to determine if/when preventive action can be taken:

> The convergence in time and space of an adversary's capability, intention, past history, opportunity, and current actions." If all these facets are not obtained and analyzed in sufficient and qualitative quantities, there will be difficulties with legal justification, moral arguments, and political and military feasibility.[88]

Overt Preventive Policy?

A question comes up as to the wisdom of whether or not to publically announce preventive policy. Some argue that a conscious decision to remain ambiguous and non-committal about prevention can be the best policy. When applied properly, such a policy would avoid direct criticism from other nations for being too aggressive, while still keeping the targeted entity sufficiently unsure of the true intentions, and thus remain effectively deterred from taking the undesired action. Others however are less concerned with the legitimacy or ―How will it make me look to the neighbors?‖ argument, and instead rely on the enhanced deterrence message an unambiguous statement makes. For the active objects of these policies, what the U.S. actually does is more important than what it says. An opposite argument exists for the majority of the international and domestic audience, not directly the object of the preventive policy however. In this case, the public message broadcast by the U.S. carries great weight. Saying the U.S. supports preventive action when necessary risks possible erosion of perceived legitimacy among observers. Of course, this deference to world opinion carries its own risks. Maintaining the moral high ground (by not having a preventive policy) and firmly gripping the concept of legitimacy can sometimes drive a policy to be more bark than bite.

Foreign Use of Deterrence Against the U.S.

The U.S. and her allies are not sole owners of deterrence tactics, techniques, and procedures. All countries and most non-state actors routinely use deterrence in varying levels as part of their overall strategies. A few vignettes where governments or non-states attempted deterrence efforts, successfully or otherwise, against the U.S. follow:

General Mohamed Farah Aideed, leader of a powerful clan in Somalia, intuitively understood U.S. and coalition aversion to casualties, especially when no monetary interests were at stake (e.g. oil, minerals). He routinely promised violent retaliation to any forces interfering with his operations, and expertly exploited the infamous ―Blackhawk Down‖ incident. Debates persist whether Aideed‘s 1993 actions continue to deter massive U.S. involvement ashore in Somalia today.

Consider Iran's ―preventive strike capability." Iran's indigenously produced Shahab-3 missiles were specifically designed as a deterrent against anyone (especially Israel or the U.S.) from striking its nuclear development facilities. Some argue that by the U.S. publically announcing a preventive policy, that action drives targeted countries, in this case Iran, to speed up their own production of a counterbalancing capability. It is a classic ―chicken or egg" argument, debating which country's action caused the build-up of weapon projection capability in a given region.

The world observed as Iraq was invaded ―before" it had obtained an effective WMD program capable of projection beyond its own borders. Had it achieved the creation of its own nuclear device first, the calculus to intervene would have been drastically reconsidered, if not altogether cancelled because of its considerable deterrent effect.

North Korea and Iran, the other two members of President George W. Bush's original *Axis of Evil* have paid close attention, and it appears that both have drawn the conclusion that owning nuclear weapons is crucial to deterring an invasion against them and preserving their own regimes.

Several countries already have official policies of prevention, including the U.S., Israel, Russia (announced after the Chechen rebel attack on the Russian school in Beslan), and Australia. If a country takes preventive action ―without" a pre-stated policy, it can only take strategic advantage of the surprise once, (like Israel did in its strike against the Iraqi nuclear reactor in 1981) because such an action then telegraphs to the world that a preemptive/preventive policy option now exists.[89] A countering consequence of retaliation must also be contemplated by the initiating country. A preemptive or

96

preventive action can actually, in some cases, be topped by a resulting counterstrike or response. The government's action or non-action calculus can be extremely difficult to assess accurately.

21st Century Deterrence Policy

Eugene Jarecki, an American documentary director noted for his film *Why We Fight*, believes that too much power corrupts the values of the U.S. democracy. He cites the farewell addresses of George Washington and Dwight D. Eisenhower to make his point: ―overgrown military establishments' were antithetical to republican liberties," and ‗We have been compelled to create a permanent armaments industry of vast proportions' and we must ‗guard against the acquisition of unwarranted influence . . . by the military-industrial complex (MIC)."[90] He believes that the National Security Act of 1947 has ―outlived its usefulness and needs to be replaced, both because it ill-equips America to meet today's security challenges and because it upset the balance of power between the branches so dangerously toward the executive."[91]

Senator John McCain states in Jarecki's film *Why We Fight*, ―Where the debate and controversy begins is, how far does the U.S. go? And when does it go from a force for good to a force of imperialism?" McCain continued, ―President Eisenhower's concern about the military-industrial complex—his words have unfortunately come true. He was worried that priorities are set by what benefits corporations as opposed to what benefits the country."[92]

After the 1991 Persian Gulf War, Paul Wolfowitz, the Undersecretary of Defense for Policy under Secretary of Defense Dick Cheney wrote an initial policy proposal known as the ―Defense Planning Guidance for the 1994-1999 Fiscal Years." According to Jarecki this document, if implemented, would ─have proved the most radical expansion of American hard power since the Truman Doctrine. It contained statements designed to ensure _a world dominated by one superpower' and to _prevent the re-emergence of a new rival".'" Jarecki characterized the document as having even more radical guidance when recommending America ─establish and protect a new order . . . deterring potential competitors from even aspiring to a larger regional or global role."[93] After the policy was prematurely leaked, it was rewritten and published by Defense Secretary Cheney in 1992, but several of its ideas remained intact and later formed many components of President George W. Bush's so-called Bush Doctrine.

The Project for the New American Century (PNAC) was founded in 1997 by neoconservatives William Kristol and Robert D. Kagan. They coined the term ─benevolent hegemon" which advocated ─resisting and where possible undermining, rising dictators and hostile ideologies . . . providing assistance to those struggling against the more extreme manifestations of human evil."[94] This is an example of symmetrical containment coming from a Reaganesque mindset, and not a typical Republican stance. President Clinton rejected PNAC's call in 1998 to overthrow Saddam Hussein on WMD grounds, but did decide to engage in the Bosnia situation, largely using Kristol and Kagan's ─benevolent hegemon" principles.[95] Jarecki believes the terrorist attack on 11 September 2001 convinced a foreign policy pseudo-isolationist president to adopt many of the policies advocated by the PNAC. Candidate George W. Bush in 2000 stated that it was not ─the role of the U.S. to go around the world and say this is the way it's got to be."[96] His key appointees once inaugurated however overwhelmingly supported PNAC's positions, and the attacks on 9/11 ensured Bush would adopt those positions as well.[97]

98

Jarecki believes the "Bush Doctrine" was so rigid that it would not even consider possible merits of the isolationist side of the debate, nor would it even tolerate debate itself, because it did not even consider debate on that topic as crucial to the country's well-being.[98]

DoD's Contribution to Current Deterrence Strategy Formulation

Responsibility for deterrence strategy formulation and orders for execution will always reside primarily within the U.S. politician's realm, but certain aspects of planning and required advice to those same politicians will remain under the purview of the Department of Defense. Refer back to the simplified definition of deterrence in the opening pages of this paper: Capability X Credibility = Deterrence. While the U.S. military's role within this definition largely relates to the "capability" variable of the formula, it would possess zero "credibility" without actual employment from time to time. Two primary categories the military's role falls within regarding deterrence strategy execution are Enabling Influence and Direct Influence.

Enabling [influence] means include:
- Global Situational Awareness (ISR)
- Command and Control (C2)
- Security Cooperation and Military Integration and Interoperability
- Deterrence Assessment, Metrics, and Experimentation

Direct [influence] means include:
- Force Projection
- Active and Passive Defenses
- Global Strike (nuclear, conventional, and non-kinetic)
- Strategic Communications[99]

DoD's enabling means usually precede its direct means for deterrence operations. For instance, ISR assets enable decision makers to gain a better understanding of enemy

99

locations and vulnerabilities. Direct means, such as strike operations, follow ISR's enabling means. A deterrence operation uses DoD enabling and direct means in ways designed to determine how an adversary's decision-making can be decisively influenced by credibly threatening to deny benefits and impose costs, plus encouraging adversary restraint."[100] If direct means are called for in a particular operation due to the failure of previous deterrence attempts (DoD, State, or otherwise), certain risks must be considered. For some situations, the direct means includes preparations for Major Combat Operations (MCO), and the preparations themselves can actually achieve the desired deterrent effect, especially if those preparations receive sufficient publicity. Depending on the adversary faced however, sometimes those MCO preparations can have the opposite effect and actually prompt the enemy's leadership toward a ―use or lose" mindset.[101] Such a scenario must be anticipated and properly war-gammed to mitigate the possibilities for unintended consequences. Some analysts point to NATO's threats to mobilize for a ground offensive in the Kosovo conflict that accelerated Milosevic's systematic offensive against his country's Muslim civilian population.

Part 3

Post-Cold War Non-State Case Studies

Somalia serves as the primary post-Cold War case study for this thesis, and provides segue for non-state terrorist organization case studies as well. A quick background on the United Nations Security Council (UNSC) authority first sets the stage. Chapter VII of the U.N. Charter deals with ―Action with Respect to Threats to the Peace, Breaches of the Peace, and Acts of Aggression," and Articles 39-42 specify how the Council may use their coercive powers. First, the Council must determine the threat to

100

peace exists, and then makes recommendations or decides what action must happen.

Additional legalese and ambiguity follows, and common USNC practice now merely

asserts that it is acting under Chapter VII, rather than referring to individual articles.[102]

Somalia

In 1991, Somalia's President Siad Barre had been leader for 21 years, when it

eventually devolved into civil war between various clans. Mid-year talks in Djibouti led

to signed Djibouti Accords and the appointment of an interim president, Ali Mahdi

Mohamed, but his rival, General Mohamed Farah Aideed, fought the accords and heavy

fighting commenced by November of 1991. Thousands of refugees were nearing

starvation and by January 1992, —the U.N. High Commissioner for Refugees (UNHCR)

reported that 140,000 Somalian refugees had reached Kenya, with another 700 arriving

each day."[103] The UNSC unanimously adopted a Chapter VII resolution by stating it was

concerned with the situation in Somalia as threatening to international peace and security

and on the _heavy loss of human life and widespread material damage resulting from the

conflict . . . and . . . its consequences on the stability and peace in [sic] the region'.[104] No

requirement for ceasefire among the warring parties was required, nor was any

authorization granted for U.N. forces to enforce anything beyond the arms embargo. The

U.N. Operation in Somalia (UNOSOM I) used 50 unarmed observers and 500 lightly

armed infantry to monitor the cease-fire between Aideed and Mohamed and to protect

U.N. personnel while delivering humanitarian supplies.[105] Ineffective mediation efforts,

worsening humanitarian conditions, and extremely slow relief deployments culminated in

October 1992. The —Secretary-General reported that almost 4.5 million of Somalia's 6

million population were threatened by severe malnutrition and related diseases. Of those, at least 1.5 million were at immediate mortal risk. An estimated 300,000 had died in the 11 months from November 1991."[106] General Aideed's first deterrence effort against UNOSOM I came later that month when his forces attacked Pakistani keepers at the Mogadishu airport and issued warnings that —any forcible UNOSOM I deployment would be met by violence."[107] Instead of immediately achieving his goal, Aideed would eventually have to face significant increases in forces, who were slowly acquiring additional missions and relaxed rules of engagement.

The U.S., prompted largely by horrific images from media coverage of the situation, offered 20,000 troops, later increased to 28,000 troops —to ensure the safe delivery of international aid" in Operation Restore Hope (also called the Unified Task Force or UNITAF). The first U.S. Marines landed with live television coverage in Somalia on 9 December 1992 as an augmentation to UNOSOM forces. The Secretary-General hailed the action by saying that the Security Council had —established a precedent in the history of the United Nations: it decided for the first time to intervene militarily for strictly humanitarian purposes."[108]

UNOSOM II forces officially took over the mission from the U.S. on 4 May 1993, and were charged with expanded nation-building mandates, including disarming the warring clans, and arresting their leaders, including Aideed. UNSCR 814 authorized inspections of weapons dumps, and on 5 June 1993, 24 Pakistani soldiers were killed while performing these weapons inspections. UNSCR 837 quickly passed with further expanded UNOSOM II's powers and authorized them to _take all necessary measures against those responsible for the armed attacks . . . to establish the effective authority of

UNOSOM II throughout Somalia, including to secure the investigation of their actions and their arrest and detention for prosecution, trial and punishment'.[109]

This defacto declaration of war against Aideed and his forces tragically led to the famous battle on 3 October 1993 that resulted in the deaths of 18 Americans, one Malaysian, and between 500-1000 Somalis.[110]

Contemporary journalist Mark Bowden vividly captured the 1993 situation in the Horn of Africa in his book *Blackhawk Down*. Among the many tactical lessons learned by the participating U.S. military elements, strategic realities were likewise illustrated. Long-term military commitment to a situation requires approval ultimately down to the general public's level, and unless a compelling case can be made to justify continued effort that causes troops to die, the U.S. will withdraw. Somalia's case in 1993, while heartbreaking, did not include a financial motive, nor was it a sufficient (in the U.S. public's mind) humanitarian reason to complete the assigned mission sets.[111]

Though the root problems remained unresolved, Somali civilians still faced extreme poverty and malnutrition, the U.S. withdrew its forces in March 1994, and the last U.N. peacekeepers left a year later on March 4, 1995.[112] RAND's study into Somalia's aftermath listed the following very familiar sounding lessons learned:

> 1. Nation-building objectives should be scaled to available forces, resources, and staying power.
> 2. Military forces need to be complemented by civil capabilities for law enforcement, economic reconstruction, and political development.
> 3. Unity of command can be as important in peace operations as in war.
> 4. There can be no economic or political development without security.[113]

As common-sense sounding these lessons seem to be, Lieutenant General Ervin J. Rokke, USAF points out in his forward to another ―lessons-learned" study about Somalia that, ―Lessons are only truly learned when we incorporate them into our planning, doctrine, tactics, and training—a process which can take some time."[114]

Lawrence Freedman asserts that principles of deterrence worked against the U.S. and the U.N. resulting from the Somalia debacle, and manifested itself the following year in Rwanda. ―There, extremist Hutus took their cues from Somalia when they murdered ten Belgian troops with the small U.N. force as a (successful) act of deterrence, before embarking on a genocidal campaign."[115]

This deterrent effect lingers even today, and may have contributed to the worsened situation in 2011's Somalia, with its ineffective African Union forces struggling against a strengthening Al Shabaab, growing piracy problems, lack of working government, refugee problems, and breeding grounds for international terrorism.

Ali Osman wrote an editorial in the online journal *Somalilandpress.com* that he believes the actions currently under consideration for Somalia are misguided, dangerous, and would actually aid al-Qaeda. Osman lists three main issues:

1. The Somali Transitional Government is not a reliable partner, is incompetent, and not interested in seeing the creation of a viable Somali Republic.

2. The African Union cannot maintain sufficient troops, even if they had a credible government to work with.

3. He characterizes the proposed influx of 15,000 U.N. soldiers to work with African Union forces as woefully inadequate and merely a ―life support US Containment policy." He explains that, ―This containment policy is not intended to help Somalia but is designed to deny the insurgents a victory and would ensure a base for US Special Operations landing if needed in the

104

future." Osman further worries that this insufficient level of —friendly" action would cause terrorist activity to expand beyond Somalia into Kenya, Djibouti, Ethiopia, and Uganda due to al-Shabaab being temporarily pushed out from their Somalia strongholds. The long-term effects would thus favor terrorist organizations, as they could easily outlast U.N. mandates.[116]

Osman then proposes a Kennan-like containment solution of his own: —Let Somalis write their own history." He claims that removal of all African Union troops and any additional U.N. troops would see the end of the corrupt Transitional Federal Government (TFG), but instead of seeing al-Qaeda or al-Shabaab rapidly filling the void, there would be a confederation of elite businessmen, moderate insurgents, and Hisbul-Islam fighting against al-Shabaab. He elaborates and warns,

> The Al-Shabab hardcore groups prefer American marines than the possibility of this scenario materializing. That is the exact reason Kampala was bombed few weeks ago to make sure more African Union —life support" troops arrive that would extend the corrupt Transitional Federal Government. The African Union troops will launch missiles into population centers every hour or so as they usually do. The later scenario guarantees Al-Qaida a safe haven and fresh recruits bent on revenge for long time to come.[117]

> The new coalition government that would emerge is not going to be [sic] rubber stamp for United States and neighboring countries. However preventing this natural organic process to take its course would be reckless and dangerous not only for Somali [sic] but for East Africa as [sic] region.[118]

Containment Characteristics Comparison

Table 2 depicts a quick comparison of Soviet era containment characteristics with the case studies of Somalia's situation in 1993, its situation since 2009, and al Qaeda. The lack of any of the chosen case studies enjoying superpower status contrasts most starkly with the example of the Soviet Union. Indeed many theorists claim containment application died along with the Soviet Union, since there are no more belligerent (or otherwise) superpowers to contain. China's growing economic, military, and sheer population size is rapidly converting the country into a superpower, and these facts may resurrect classical containment in the minds of these critics.

The second factor, showing whether either side issued a capitulation demand is more difficult to analyze. Among containment's central tenets is its reliance on a large degree of patience. Rather than demand the Soviet Union immediately withdraw from its possessions following WWII, the U.S. deliberately settled on a policy designed to contain the USSR from gaining additional global influence with the understanding it could eventually outlast their ability to carry on. Aideed's Somalia was an example of the U.S. being effectively deterred from pursuing an outcome that would likely cost too much blood and treasure, with little to zero monetary or other tangible return on investment. The piracy situation in Somalia from 2009 forward has no demand for capitulation on either side, for different reasons. The U.S. has no single entity to demand capitulation from, as the pirates largely report to a variety of clans with no oversight by a coherent government. The pirates, for their part, are not in a position of demanding the coalition cease and desist prosecuting them.

None of the illustrated examples has set a specific timeline for accomplishing their goals, but this does not mean the measure is irrelevant. An expanded containment relevancy study with Iran included as a case study would show a ―Yes‖ to this question, and could therefore skew the policymaker's decision making. As previously mentioned, containment requires patience. If the containment target's leadership pursues his end state in accordance with a timeline, patience may cease to be an option. Potential WMD proliferation also guides the policymaker's course. While this thesis does not analyze

106

ratios of WMD usage potential to relative degree of U.S. military response, it seems logical to assume more effort and assign priority is assigned to entities threatening WMD employment. Therefore, evidence pointing toward Al Qaeda's desire to acquire and use WMD against the U.S. justifies more resources to disrupt (contain), dismantle, and defeat its network than it does to do the same against Somali pirates. The final chart factor describing the target's governmental status, while interesting, is probably hobbled by brevity of included case studies. Relevancy would be enhanced by inclusion of additional examples.

Table 2.   Factor Comparison of Cold War to Thesis Case Studies

	Superpower Opponent?	Capitulation Demand by U.S. or Opponent?	Specific Timeline to Accomplish Goals?	Is Threat Primarily Conventional or WMD? Deterrence type/level:	State, Failed State, or Non-State?
Soviet Union	Yes	No (U.S.)	No	WMD/parity	State
Somalia-1993	No	Yes (Aideed)	No	Conventional/ strong regionally	Failed State
Somalia-2009	No	No	No	Conventional/ strong on land-weak at sea	Failed State
al Qaeda	No	Yes? (Both?)	No	Conventional (WMD emerging)	Non-State

Source: Created by author.

Other possible variables include whether the U.S. was operating with a détente mindset. Some theorists believe détente, while de-escalatory by nature, might actually prolong the desired end state from occurring. Conciliatory stances by Nixon, and especially Carter, resulted in further Soviet expansion and eventual invasion of Afghanistan, whereas the principled tough stand of Reagan saw much more fruitful results. Could a similar détente policy toward today's adversaries have similar unintended consequences?

Another potential component of modern containment strategy concerns whether to make preventive policy public. This fits more into deterrence policy, but it could also fit the Somalia piracy containment situation. For instance, announcing that pirate camps in Somalia were subject to unannounced attacks, and occasional follow-through of that threat, could help contain the overall piracy problem. Like all other containment scenarios, it does not directly address the underlying causes of the problem, though it can greatly contribute to limiting (or containing) its spread. An official and well-publicized preventive policy against piracy may be a partial solution to the Somalia piracy situation. Current reactive policy treats symptoms, but neglects the actual cause of piracy. Non-state terrorist organizations should be subject to a similar preventive policy, with all nations under notice that the U.S. and a ‑coalition of the willing" will pursue them wherever and whenever detected.

Global politics is often likened to high stakes poker. Credibility is only achieved if it is backed up with real ability and willingness to carry out the threatened action if the targeted country/entity does not back away from the action it is contemplating. Once the figurative line in the sand has been drawn, the ‑game" intensifies. Which, if any, competitor is bluffing? Will one side blink first, or will hostilities result?

When evaluating threat, one must consider interests of the threatening entity. This gets at the heart of ‑intent," which is more important than the study of capability. Of course, capability is crucial as well, but if the hostile application of a capability is not within the belligerent's interest (intent), the analyst may conclude (usually safely) that the threat is not imminent. Intent unfortunately, is often the most difficult intelligence product to acquire both quickly and accurately, but if it is actually attained, it will factor heavily into deliberations whether preemptive or preventive action should be taken.

The law of unintended consequences goes both ways. It affects actions and inaction. It must be accounted for either way. Iraq and WWII are examples of each.

Table 3 compares six additional Cold War containment factors with thesis case studies. Like table 2, it suffers somewhat from a short list of cases, but interesting information can be gleaned nonetheless.

All studied cases enjoyed high relative degrees of non-partisan support. Different Cold War presidential administrations employed styles of containment (namely symmetrical and asymmetrical), but overarching goals remained constant. Likewise, modern U.S. presidents shared remarkable unity of effort regarding the case study examples. An expanded list would show differences.

The U.S. public was extremely patient throughout the Cold War with its presidents' various containment policies, and remains so throughout the prosecution of the long war against Al Qaeda and its affiliates. Table 3's only "No" answer applied to the situation in Somalia in 1993. Without presenting detailed evidence, this thesis contents itself to postulating that the patience deficiency was largely due to Somalia's perceived lack of economic impact on world affairs, as well as the common belief that no Somali was worth the life of a U.S. military member.

The chart's next factor compared degree of global cooperation. While all are marked "multilateral," the amount of time varies. The collective threat against the free world during the Cold War was greater, thus the long-term commitment to containment policy is not surprising.

Horrible humanitarian conditions in Somalia during the early 1990s was sufficient to unite the world in its initial efforts, but hostile and deadly responses toward the Coalition's operations resulted in overall mission failure.

The factor or factors responsible for triggering a U.S. or coalition response is shown on the chart next, and is listed in priority order. The Soviet Union, with all its faults, was not listed as a terrorist state, thus leaving the "T" out of its corresponding chart block. All other factors strongly applied however.

Aideed's 1993 Somalia featured multiple clans fighting internally with each other and any international force that dared enter his span of control, but Al Shabaab and other Somalia terrorist organizations did not yet exist. WMD was not a factor in Somalia, and the world could not expect an economic return on investment either, so the only applicable reason to trigger a coalition response was moral, due to extreme humanitarian suffering.

The U.S. supports the African Union and the United Nations' efforts in Somalia today, but does not maintain a presence ashore. The main global efforts today are focused on the piracy situation and the resulting economic impact, as well as containment of a growing terrorism breeding ground. The absence of large ground commitment means the moral rationale for assisting Somalia lacks sufficient global persuasive power, and is likely to remain that way unless an economic argument can be attached.

The last evaluated factor shows the weight of the traditional national instruments of power, when applied to the Soviet Union and the selected case studies. Only the Soviet Union received the full application of DIME, thus bolstering the case some make against containment's continued applicability post-Cold War. This is largely because non-state entities lack diplomatic status (the ―D‖ of DIME), and information campaigns (represented in DIME by the ―I‖) are more challenging. An expanded study including China, Iran, and North Korea would perhaps refute this conclusion however.

Table 3.   Cold War Containment Analysis

	Unity of Effort (Non-Partisan)?	Long-Term Public Patience?	Allied Support: Unilateral or Multilateral?	Response Trigger? (WMD, Economic, Terrorist, or Moral?)	DIME weight?
Soviet Union	Yes (with Sym/Assym differences)	Yes	Multilateral	WMD, E, M	D,I,M,E
Somalia-1993	Yes	No	Multilateral (short term)	M	I,M
Somalia-2009	Yes	Yes	Multilateral (long term)	E, T	M
Al Qaeda	Yes	Yes	Multilateral, but global commitment fading	E, T, M, (WMD emerging)	I, M

Source: Created by author.

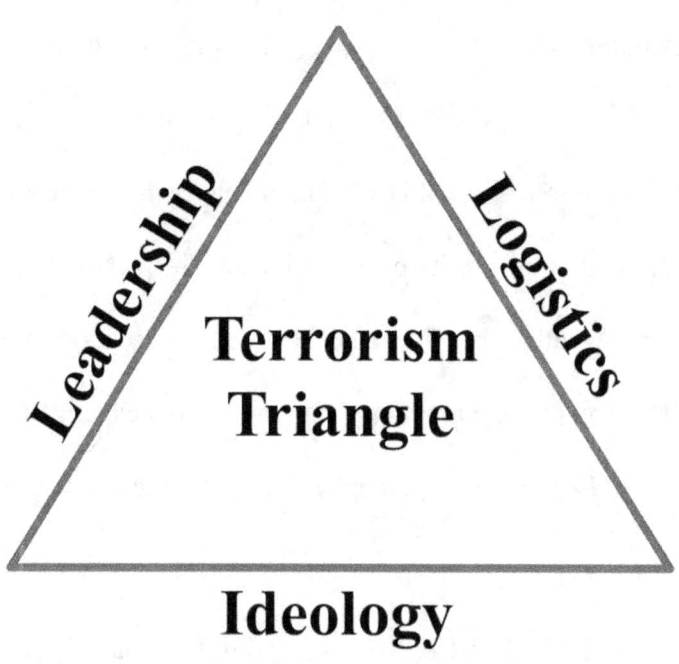

Figure 1.   Non-State Terrorist Organizations (Analysis & Strategy Formulation)
Source: Created by author.

The terrorism phenomenon, simply illustrated in the figure above, shows three main components: Leadership, Logistics, and Ideology. Permanent removal of any individual component will lead to cessation of terrorism, at least from that particular source. Not all components are equally vulnerable, thus driving tactical and strategic approaches to handling the problem.

Dr. Cronin's list of the six most common means that terrorism campaigns end fit into the terrorism triangle model as well. Number one on her list is decapitation, which includes either the killing or capture of the particular group's leader.[119] Smaller less organized terrorist groups are more vulnerable to this option, as more established organizations likely have predetermined succession plans to execute in just such a contingency. The 1 May 2011 special forces raid in Pakistan that resulted in Osama bin

112

Laden's death, while psychologically huge, is not likely to result in al Qaida's near term

demise. The U.S. government understood this when announcing bin Laden's death

however, and carefully chose its words in an effort to pursue more than solely a

decapitation course. President Obama's speech to the nation and world reiterated that,

> the United States is not - and never will be - at war with Islam. I've made clear,
> just as President Bush did shortly after 9/11, that our war is not against Islam. Bin
> Laden was not a Muslim leader; he was a mass murderer of Muslims. Indeed, Al-
> Qaeda has slaughtered scores of Muslims in many countries, including our own.
> So his demise should be welcomed by all who believe in peace and human
> dignity.[120]

President Obama invoked Cronin's method number four, ―Failure: Imploding,

Provoking a Backlash, or Becoming Marginalized," which neatly fits into the Terrorism

Triangle's base, Ideology.[121]

The authors of the 5th edition of *American National Security* warn that military

forces must be given achievable goals before being committed to action, because to do

otherwise risks long-term global credibility. Credibility, as already discussed, remains

vital to the overall effectiveness of deterrence operations. Credibility is equally important

in implementing a nation's containment strategy. ―Without clear and realistic military

objectives, the employment of U.S. ground forces can vitiate the very effectiveness of the

military instrument sought by policymakers, threaten foreign policy objectives, and erode

confidence in U.S. capabilities."[122]

Tasks a military can reasonably perform within the terrorism triangle typically

focus on leadership and logistic targets, though with creative information operations

planning and execution, they can occasionally affect the ideology plank as well. With

rare exception however, military operations against non-states and phenomenon like

terrorism and piracy must include other agency support in order to achieve enduring

113

success. Military operations often create exploitable gaps, but without State, Treasury, Agriculture, Commerce, and the ―whole of government approach" rapidly advancing when such opportunities present themselves, long-term policy effectiveness is doubtful.

Dr. Paul Pillar identified in his book, *Terrorism and U.S. Foreign Policy*, the relatively constant list of counterterrorism tenets:

-Make no concessions to terrorists and strike no deals.
-Bring terrorists to justice for their crimes
-Isolate and apply pressure on states that sponsor terrorism to force them to change their behavior.
-Bolster the counterterrorist capabilities of those countries that work with the United States and require assistance.[123]

He questions however if the ―no deals" mandate may miss opportunities to decrease terrorist attacks on the U.S. While not quite advocating appeasement, Pillar's mere question raises the consideration that rigid policy enforcement under all circumstances may occasionally miss opportunities.

Pillar recognizes that effective counterterrorism strategy requires multiple elements. Among them are targeting the terrorist organization's roots (conditions and issues), capabilities, intentions, and defenses.[124] He continues that the strategy must coordinate the use of counterterrorism instruments including ―diplomacy, the criminal justice system, interdiction of financial assets, military force, and intelligence, as well as possible use of the intelligence apparatus for covert action."[125]

Unique Non-State Containment Challenges

Philip Seib wrote an article in the May-June 2008 edition of *Military Review* about how al-Qaeda skillfully uses media and technology to get its message out, train its personnel, conduct information operations, recruit globally, and wage cyberspace warfare. He points to the major impediment to containing organizations like al-Qaeda: their lack of recognizable state sponsorship that could be held accountable for their actions. ―Lacking a tangible homeland—other than, perhaps, scattered outposts in the wilds of Waziristan—al-Qaeda has established itself as a virtual state that communicates with its ―citizens" and cultivates an even larger audience through masterful use of the media, with a heavy reliance on the Internet." He continues by explaining why Osama bin Laden played only a minor role in al-Qaeda's continuing jihad: ―For every conventional video performance by bin Laden that appears on *Al-Jazeera* and other major television outlets, there are hundreds of online videos that proselytize, recruit, and train the al-Qaeda constituency."[126] Legitimate debate continues regarding whether media coverage helps or hinders terrorism. Terrorists rely on news organizations getting their message to wide audiences, yet that message, while temporarily advertising their overall goals, also graphically depicts their brutal methods, often leading to public demands for their punishment.

Two famous voices making the argument that the media assists terrorists are former British Prime Minister Margaret Thatcher and Israeli Prime Minister Benjamin Netanyahu. Thatcher's now famous metaphor compares the media as ―the oxygen of publicity on which [terrorists] depend." Netanyahu takes it up a notch and maintains that, ―unreported, terrorist acts would be like the proverbial tree falling in the silent forest." Bruce Hoffman, author of the book *Inside Terrorism,* amplifies Thatcher and Netanyahu's argument: ―The obvious implication being made in all these assertions is that if the terrorists could somehow be _starved' of the publicity on which they _thrive', both their malignant influence and the frequency with which they act would be greatly

115

reduced."[127] The other side of the argument points out that media coverage on terrorism is seldom positive. A RAND study conducted from 1988 to 1989 sought to determine how acts of terrorism affect public opinion. The study included 1985's TWA hijacking and the Palestine Liberation Front's hijacking of Italian cruise ship *Achille Lauro*, and therefore the public's awareness was high. Despite the media's continual and often intense attention to terrorist activities over a period of years, however, the RAND study found that public approval for terrorists was effectively zero" [emphasis added]."[128]

Both arguments have merit and therefore deserve further study when formulating an anti-terrorism policy, be it containment or some other model. Further discussion on this subject follows in chapter 5.

Recommendation: Step 1-Recognize media's symbiotic relationship with terrorism. Step 2-Exploit. It remains debatable whether to conduct this exploitation openly as published policy, or to pursue a more clandestine route.

Paul Wilkinson, Professor of International Relations and Director, Centre for the Study of Terrorism and Political Violence, at the University of St Andrews in Scotland writes about terrorism policy options. He treats terrorism as a legal problem that demands justice in an international law sense, but simultaneously recognizes the occasional need for military response.

> The response of the liberal democratic state at international level should be firm and courageous, but always within the rule of law. Massive military retaliation against states or groups involved in terrorism will only tend to substitute the even greater evil of war, with its attendant massive loss of life and destruction, in place of the lesser evil of terrorism. Yet equally it is essential to avoid cowardly under-reaction and surrender. Terrorism is a fundamental attack on human rights, and the international community has a moral as well as a legal duty to combat this international scourge of the innocent. [G]overnments must in all circumstances try to avoid, on the one hand, appeasement or weakness in response to terrorism, and

116

on the other, draconian overreaction that would hand the terrorists a victory by suspending democracy in the name of defending it.[129]

Challenges to International Counter-Terrorism Cooperation

Wilkinson's summarized theory explaining why democratic countries continue to have extreme difficulty in achieving cooperation against terrorism follows:

1. Internal security and laws remain totally sovereign to individual countries
2. Many states have yet to become victims of terrorism, and therefore do not experience the same sense of urgency as those who have
3. Economic linkages to pro-terrorist states often prevent unified action.
4. Some states –buy security though appeasement"
5. Some states maintain double standards, and regard some terrorists as –freedom fighters," (e.g. Irish Americans attitudes to the IRA, the French attitudes to Armenian terrorists, and the Greek attitude to the Palestinian Liberation Organization)
6. Pervasive terrorist propaganda convincing many defeatists that –democracies can do nothing to defeat terrorism.[130]

Counter Terrorism Policy Formulation

Wilkinson believes all countries must stand together against terrorism, regardless of form, if any cohesive and effective counter terrorism policy can hope to form. They must adopt the clear principle that _one democracy's terrorist is another democracy's terrorist.'"[131]

Daniel Whiteneck, believes certain terrorist organizations like al-Qaeda may actually seek escalation from the U.S. in response to an attack, especially if it also achieves desired effects on Muslim governments and societies. –An adversary that prefers escalation regardless of the consequences cannot be deterred."[132] He therefore advocates constructing a deterrence strategy aimed at moderate elements within the targeted terrorist networks, with the goal of severing much of that network's logistics aid, while aiming the strategy against the general population that either directly supports the network or passively tolerates its presence. –Making the general population aware that they might pay a large proportion of the _costs' of a terrorist attack against the U.S. may support the large deterrent aims."[133] Such a policy risks responding to a population that may not be guilty and terrorists knowing this will likely seek states with weak governments or lack of resources to adequately police themselves, to use as personal shields against retribution. Any policy would obviously also require legality and wide support if it hopes to achieve legitimacy.

Tailored Deterrence

Previous U.S. containment strategies and individual deterrence policies heavily focused on WMD, but ―tailored deterrence" goes beyond the traditional nuclear triad defenses ―to the full range of military capabilities, presence, and cooperation, as well as diplomatic, informational, and economic instruments." Tailoring deterrence to specific actors and situations requires a ―continuing set of comprehensive country or group deterrence assessments."[134] Meeting such a requirement mandates either significant increases in the intelligence community's resources, drastic restructuring, or both.

Bunn believes dissuasion plays a critical role, just as deterrence does. She carefully distinguishes the two terms:

> While deterrence is focused on convincing an adversary not to undertake acts of aggression, dissuasion is aimed at convincing a potential adversary not to compete with the United States or go down an undesirable path, such as acquiring, enhancing, or increasing threatening capabilities.[135]

To simplify, aggression can be deterred, while acquisition or improvement of a capability can be dissuaded. Because both rely on influencing decisions of target actors, comprehensive strategies must be developed to handle both situations.[136]

Refer back to figure 1 to see how attacking one or more planks of the Terrorism Triangle can assist crafting a more effective containment or deterrence strategy.

International Deterrence and Containment Efforts
in Somali Piracy Situation

The international maritime shipping community, tired of Somali pirates increasingly successful at capturing their vessels, cargo, and crews, eventually convinced their governments that something had to be done to remedy the situation. Rather than a jointly coordinated U.N. reaction however, multiple countries and organizations formed their own unique responses. Each entity brought its own biases, rules of engagement, strategies, and desired end states. Some mutually benefited the global community, while others were strictly limited to supporting its own sponsor country. Some countries' policies show an orientation toward deterring future pirate attacks, while others seem content to containing piracy rates and operating areas to current levels. Other countries, like India, appear to have taken the gloves off, and are aggressively, and often lethally, prosecuting any pirates they come across.

Currently, maritime forces working against Somalia piracy include assets from the following organizations and independent countries:

1. European Union Naval Forces Somalia (EUNAVFOR), also known as Operation Atalanta; note: Norway, though not part of the European Union, is also contributing ships and personnel to Operation Atalanta's misson. Other non-EU nations including Croatia, Ukraine, and Montenegro also support EUNAVFOR.

119

2. Combined Maritime Forces, coordinated in Bahrain by the U.S. 5th Fleet, consists of several subordinate combined task forces (CTFs), each with varying mission statements, areas of responsibility, and degrees of active support against Somali pirates. Participating countries lead these CTFs, with rotations conducted on an agreed-upon schedule.

3. NATO has its own mission and assets deployed in action against Somalia piracy.

4. China-Independent deployer.

5. Russia-Independent deployer.

6. India-Independent deployer.

7. Taiwan-Independent deployer.

8. Iran-Independent deployer.[137]

Coordination attempts occur among the disparate anti-piracy operations, and a fair amount of successful interdictions, rescues, and foiled piracy attempts can be credited to their overall efforts.

Root causes of Somali piracy are rarely addressed adequately however. EUNAVFOR's official mission statement for Operation Atalanta says its forces will —contribute [emphasis added] to":

- the protection of vessels of the WFP delivering food aid to displaced persons in Somalia;

- the protection of vulnerable vessels cruising off the Somali coast, and the deterrence, prevention and repression of acts of piracy and armed robbery off the Somali coast;

- in addition, ATALANTA shall contribute to the monitoring of fishing activities off the coast of Somalia.[138]

To analyze these statements a bit further, first the EU does not expect to accomplish any of its missions alone. It merely states, rather ambiguously, that its forces will contribute in its accomplishment. Next, the "monitoring of fishing activities" is particularly weak. Many Somali pirates began as legitimate fishermen, trying to seek out a meager living for their families. The Barre regime collapsed, and any semblance of a Coast Guard collapsed along with it. The lack of maritime law enforcement led to exploitation of Somalia's rich fishing areas by well-equipped foreign fishing fleets, especially from Japan, Russia, and China. Because Somalia could no longer support its own fishing fleet, several local anglers armed themselves, and fought back. Quickly surmising that demanding ransoms for captured foreign fishing boats and their crews was more lucrative than legitimately fishing for themselves, the new "profession" of piracy was born. So, for the EU to "monitor" fishing activities, without actually enforcing legitimate Somali fishery claims, loses credibility and dwindles chances of forming an effective piracy containment strategy.

Karsten von Hoesslin, writes and lectures about maritime security issues, and is particularly active with efforts to contain piracy off the Horn of Africa. He concurs that

> the international maritime shipping and fishing communities must also share responsibility because their intrusion into Somali territorial waters and Exclusive Economic Zone have provoked a vigilante-style response from coastal-based warlords. This is the main reason for the dramatic recent upsurge in piracy.[139]

Each participating anti-piracy coalition or individual country touts its accomplishments to justify its continuing mission. Operation ATALANTA boasts,

> Since escorts began in late 2007, not a single ship carrying WFP food to ports in Somalia has been attacked by pirates. Under the EU NAVFOR operation, which started in December 2008, and until November 2010, WFP has delivered more than 480,000 metric tons of food into Somalia through Mogadishu, Merka, Bossaso, Berbera ports.[140]

Iranian state-run media quoted the Iranian commander of naval forces regarding

its anti-piracy efforts,

> The main reason for dispatching this fleet of warships to the Gulf of Aden was to combat piracy and to spread the Islamic Republic's message of peace to neighboring states and other countries in the Gulf of Aden. Over the past 18 months, the Islamic Republic has dispatched warship and support frigates to the Gulf of Aden which have escorted 400 trade ships and tankers," he added without elaborating on whether all the vessels were Iranian."[141]

Iran believes its independent policing action against piracy helps its international

image. Official media cited Iran's navy as "the strongest" and the best equipped and

staffed force in the Persian Gulf and the Sea of Oman," and stressed, "Iran and littoral

states around the two bodies of water did not need outside help in safeguarding the

region."[142]

The following passage from Chinese on-line newspaper *Global Times* provides

relatively candid rationale for supporting their independent anti-piracy efforts in the Horn

of Africa:

> China's anti-piracy mission in the waters of the Gulf of Aden is related to the country's African strategy, a Chinese scholar told the Global Times Sunday. "The diplomatic success in Africa will subsequently strengthen China's role in multilateral relations in the world arena," Xu Weizhong, deputy director at the Institute of West Asian and African Studies of the China Institutes of Contemporary International Relations, said. "Given the potential penetration of major powers' influence in counter-piracy operations in Somalia, China's active engagement will guarantee the maintenance of the current diplomatic advantages in Africa," he added. Xu's words came after China upgraded its anti-piracy mission in the gulf region. According to a statement released on the website of China's Ministry of National Defense, China's naval escort route was further extended 50 nautical miles (92.6 kilometers) eastward starting from January 1. "China's involvement in fighting piracy illustrates the nation's commitment to preserving international maritime security and world peace," Xu said. "Furthermore, participation in anti-piracy in Somali waters serves as a testing opportunity for China's naval forces and its capability to project long-range combat operations," Xu added.[143]

Russians, like all anti-piracy participants, frequently justify their on-going

mission to their countrymen.

> [The] Russian-secured corridor is much longer than safety zones of other multinational forces. No vessels have been captured in [the] Russian security corridor, in contrast to international corridor[s] where another protection method is used – area patrols. Our warships several times successfully repelled pirate assaults, [and] some pirates were detained. Since Dec 24, 2010 these those are performed by Pacific Fleet's large ASW ship *Admiral Vinogradov* which has escorted 52 foreign and 22 Russian-crewed vessels. In 2011 it is planned to conduct about 5 anti-piracy missions by means of Northern and Pacific fleets.[144]

Missing from all these posted comments is the lack of a jointly coordinated anti-

piracy containment strategy. While easy to claim that their true motivation solely lies

with ensuring safe passage of their flagged country's merchant ships (which is partially

true), the Indian Ocean's increasing importance demands immediate and sustained

presence from the ocean-going global community. Countries not participating perceive

they will be left behind.

Refer back to table 3's depiction of relative values of economic and moral factors

when determining an initial or sustained response in a given situation.

Economic Relative Relevancy

Compare the current situation in Libya with that of Somalia. Libya's oil and

global market implications prompted Western military force response against Qaddafi's

integrated air defense forces, his military aircraft, and his mechanized ground forces, with

official U.N. and Arab-world sanction, in a matter of weeks. Somalia, on the other hand,

with practically zero wealth to offer the West, continues to languish without significant

Western military intervention, since the pullout of UNOSOM II forces in 1995.

Inadequate, poorly trained, ill-disciplined African Union troops conduct occasional operations, but stand virtually no chance to remedy the situation in Somalia. The multiple Coalition task forces and independent deployers charged with responding to the ongoing scourge of piracy are not given the tools or authority to attack piracy's root causes. Given this reality, containment seems the most viable course of action.

Containment Hypothesis

So how then does containment work? Chapter 3 explained the methodology, and step one calls for creating a hypothesis. Chapter 4's analysis results yielded multiple possible components, but the factors constantly observed have more promise than those variably present. Extracts from the Cold War presidential administration containment policies, various war theories, and the selected case studies suggest the following hypothetical formula for calculating containment's effectiveness:

$$\frac{(\text{Patience} + \text{Economic Benefit} + \text{Manageable Risk})(\text{Unity of Effort})(\text{Allied Support})}{(\text{Capitulation Demand})(\text{Deterrence})}$$

Disclaimer

Permanent numerical and factors assignment to this formula makes no sense because of the almost infinite unconsidered variables, each with incalculable individual weighting. The formula remains useful however due to its rudimentary illustrative properties when considering containment policy formulation and recommendations by planner staff, and therefore serves as a planning tool. An accurate predictive tool requires much more research and inclusion of other factors, but this basic model should give the conversation and debate a good head start.

Formula Mechanics

All factors are measured on a scale of one to three, with three being the highest. Factors on the numerator side of the equation are items affecting the "good guys," with higher numbers leading to better chances of overall success. Denominator numbers are factors affecting the "bad guys," or targets of the containment or deterrence effort. Higher numbers there adversely affect the "good guy's" chances of success. The exact predictability and time required to achieve success cannot be ascertained from this model, however an assessment of each formula factor will assist the overall planning process. Examples of what scores a three follow:

A Patience score of 3 is awarded to the Cold War, since it is the longest period that the collective assets of the U.S. has committed itself to any containment strategy.

An Economic Benefit score of 3 could be assigned to any situation where lack of containment action would result in significant loss of capital.

A Manageable Risk score of 3 means the U.S. has the maximum ability to manage the risks of fully prosecuting the target. The target is easily identified and separated from non-targeted population, and is assessed sufficiently vulnerable. The assessed retaliatory capability of the target is insufficient to deter U.S. action.

A Unity of Effort score of 3 is given when the issue is largely non-partisan in nature, has public broad support, and inter-agency coordination occurs at a high level.

An Allied Support score of 3 is given when significant and sustained allied support occurs without undue coercion.

A Capitulation Demand score of 3 is awarded to a target entity that issues demands for the prosecuting country or coalition to cede territory, authority, property, or manpower above what they started with. A score of 2 then simply has the target entity demanding preservation of the status quo, and a score of 1 means no capitulation demand by the target entity was issued.

A Deterrence score of 3 is given to a target that enjoys both parity level capability with its opponent, as well as demonstrated or assessed credibility for actually using their capability should perceived red lines get crossed.

For sake of argument, the thesis postulates temporary number values using 1993 and 2009 Somalia situations, with the following scale:

Aideed's Somalia

Patience=1 (No concerted efforts to ensure long-term commitment to the Somalia situation were undertaken by the American public, Congress, or the White House, though the involvement period did cross over from the Bush to Clinton administrations). Economic Benefit=1 (The piracy problem had not yet emerged, and Somalia offered little economic benefit to the U.S., though regional stability generally provided economic growth opportunity).

Manageable Risk=3 (Aideed's Somalia presented zero existential threat to the U.S. outside his borders).

Unity of Effort=1 (Mission creep from original humanitarian operations to eventual clan overthrow attempts; lack of unified U.S. public or governmental clarity toward mission).

Allied Support=3 (Significant assistance from non-US assets were present, though coordination and Rules of Engagement [ROE] differences hindered operations).

Capitulation Demand by Target=2 (Aideed issued direct threats and demands to Coalition).

Deterrence by Target=2* (Aideed's threats achieved credibility with his successful attacks against coalition targets, and infamous —Blackhawk Down" incident. *deterrence = capability multiplied by credibility

These factors, with valuations admittedly debatable, when plugged into the proposed formula, yield the following:

$$\frac{(\text{Patience} + \text{Economic Benefit} + \text{Manageable Risk})(\text{Unity of Effort})(\text{Allied Support})}{\text{Capitulation Demand by Target} + \text{Deterrence Capability by Target}}$$

$$\frac{(1+1+3)(1)(3)}{2+2}$$

Results: 15/4, which reduces to 3.75.

3.75, without any established units or reference points, demands a further example for comparison, hence the Somalia piracy situation since 2009.

Piracy 2009

Patience=3 (The U.S. response remains largely composed of naval assets that would already be present in the 5th Fleet Area of Responsibility (AOR), though admittedly not necessarily off the Horn of Africa. Minimal extra cost to defense requirements provokes little public criticism of anti-piracy funding, and occasional spectacular events [e.g. Maersk Alabama] actually increase public's patience with overall effort).

Economic Benefit=3 (Decrease in increased maritime costs associated with piracy result in cheaper goods for U.S. and global consumers).

127

Manageable Risk=3 (Pirates present small risk to military response forces while underway, though land-based operations would change this calculus).

Unity of Effort=2 (Multiple organizations with conflicting ROE, missions, and motivations prevent this from achieving a score of 3).

Allied Support=2 (Significant assets from multiple countries are present, but vast areas requiring coverage still outweigh available resources).

Capitulation=1 (Pirates are not in a position to demand capitulation from countries or their militaries, though they do demand and receive ransom payments more often than they do not).

Deterrence=1 (Pirates' weaponry and occasional threats to attack military targets does little to deter a vastly superior coalition military response, though as mentioned with the manageable risk category, this calculus would change with land-based operations).

The values, thus inserted into the formula:

$$\frac{(3+3+3)(2)(2)}{(1+1)}$$

Results: 18

Interpretation

Higher numbers predict higher chance of containment policy's success, though they offer no timetable for when that success will occur. The planner's goal will be to include actions that positively affect the assessed values of the factors in the numerator of the formula, while minimizing the assessed valuations of factors in the denominator whenever possible.

Somalia 1993 resulted in a number of 3.75, while the piracy situation off Somalia‛s shores as of 2009 resulted with a number of 18. These results require further research and refinement, but obviously point toward the modern piracy example as being more aligned with the goals and capabilities of a containment strategy.

---

[1]John L. Gaddis, *The Cold War: A New History* (New York, NY: The Penguin Press, 2005), 25-6.

[2]Ibid.

[3]Ibid., 27.

[4]John L. Gaddis, *Strategies of Containment* (New York, NY: Oxford University Press, 1982), 329.

[5]Gaddis, *The Cold War*, 29.

[6]Ibid.

[7]Gaddis, *Strategies of Containment*, 21.

[8]Ibid.

[9]Ibid., 22.

[10]Ibid.

[11]Ibid.

[12]Ibid.

[13]Ibid.

[14]Ibid., 380.

[15]Ibid.

[16]Ibid., 381.

[17]Ibid.

[18]Ibid., 382.

[19]Ibid.

[20]W. B. Pickett, ed., "George F. Kennan and the Origins of Eisenhower's New Look: an Oral History of Project Solarium" (Monograph Series Number 1, Princeton Institute for International and Regional Studies, Princeton, NJ, 2004), 2.

[21]Ibid., 9.

[22]Ibid., 3.

[23]Ibid., 4.

[24]Ibid.

[25]Ibid., 9-10.

[26]Amos A. Jordan, William J. Taylor, Jr., and Michael J. Mazarr, *American National Security,* 5th ed. (Baltimore, MD: The Johns Hopkins University Press, 1999), 262.

[27]Ibid., 263.

[28]Gaddis, *Strategies of Containment*, 218.

[29]Ibid.

[30]Ibid., 219.

[31]Ibid., 210.

[32]Ibid.

[33]Ibid., 212.

[34]Ibid., 273.

[35]Ibid.

[36]Ibid., 274.

[37]Ibid., 281.

[38]Ibid., 275.

[39]Ibid., 276.

[40]Ibid., 278.

[41]Ibid., 282.

[42]Ibid., 287.

[43]Ibid., 273.

[44]Ibid., 285.

[45]Ibid., 343.

[46]Ibid.

[47]Ibid., 344.

[48]Ibid., 345.

[49]Ibid.

[50]Gaddis, *The Cold War*, 362.

[51]Ibid., 357.

[52]Ibid., 359.

[53]Ibid., 355.

[54]Ibid., 364.

[55]Ibid., 367.

[56]Ibid., 369.

[57]Ibid., 367.

[58]Ibid.

[59]Ibid., 375-6.

[60]Ibid., 376.

[61]Ibid.

[62]John J. Mearsheimer, *The Tragedy of Great Power Politics* (New York: W.W. Norton & Company, Inc., 2001), 8.

[63]Ibid., 10-11.

[64]Ibid.

[65]Charles L. Glaser, ―Realists as Optimists: Cooperation as Self-Help,"
International Security 19, no. 3 (Winter 1994-1995), http://www.jstor.org/pss/2539079
(accessed 13 March 2010), 50-90.

[66]Mearsheimer, 9.

[67]Michael Walzer, *Arguing about War* (New Haven, CT: Yale University Press,
2004), ix.

[68]Ibid., x.

[69]Ibid., xi.

[70]Ibid.

[71]Ibid. xiii.

[72]Ibid., 9.

[73]Ibid., 6.

[74]Ibid.

[75]Ibid., 39.

[76]DoD, Joint Pub 5-0, GL-11.

[77]Ibid., 41.

[78]Ibid.

[79]Marcus Luttrell, *Lone Survivor* (New York: Little, Brown and Company, 2007),
200-08.

[80]Waltzer, 45.

[81]Ibid., 46.

[82]Ibid., 48-9.

[83]Colin S. Gray, ―The Implications of Preemptive and Preventive War Doctrines: A Reconsidation" (Monograph, Strategic Studies Institute, Carlisle Barracks, PA, 2007), v-vi.

[84]Alan Dershowitz, *Preemption:A Knife that Cuts Both Ways* (New York, NY: W.W. Norton & Company, Inc., 2006), 129.

[85]Ibid., 159.

[86]Ibid., 161.

[87]Ibid., 162.

[88]Ibid.

[89]Ibid., 167.

[90]Eugene Jarecki, *The American Way of War: Guided Missiles, Misguided Men, and a Republic in Peril* (New York, NY: Free Press, 2008), 4.

[91]Ibid., 273.

[92]Ibid.

[93]Ibid., 12.

[94]Ibid., 13.

[95]Ibid.

[96]Ibid., 14.

[97]Ibid., 15.

[98]Ibid., 10.

[99]Department of Defense, *Deterrence Operations Joint Operating Concept (DO JOC)*, Version 2.0, (Omaha, NE: U.S. Strategic Command, 2006), 6.

[100]Ibid.

[101]Ibid., 10.

[102]Simon Chesterman, *Just War or Just Peace?: Humanitarian Intervention and International Law* (New York, NY: Oxford University Press, 2001), 124-5.

[103]Ibid., 140.

[104]Ibid.

[105]James Dobbins, John G. McGinn, Keith Crane, Seth G. Jones, Rollie Lal, Andrew Rathmell, Rachel Swanger, and Anga Timilsina, *America's Role in Nation-Building: From Germany to Iraq* (Santa Monica, CA: RAND, 2003), 55.

[106]Chesterman, 141.

[107]Dobbins et al., 56.

[108]Chesterman, 141.

[109]Ibid.

[110]Ibid., 143.

[111]Mark Bowden, *Blackhawk Down* (New York, NY: Signet Books, 1999), 427.

[112]Chesterman, 143.

[113]Dobbins et al., 69.

[114]Kenneth Allard, *Somalia Operations: Lessons Learned* (Washington, DC: National Defense University Press, 2004), xi.

[115]Lawrence Freedman, *Deterrence* (Cambridge, UK: Polity Press, 2004), 125.

[116]Ali Osman, "Op-Ed-Somalia: The Wrong Strategy," *Somalialand Press.com*, http://somalilandpress.com/op-ed-somalia-the-wrong-strategy-17410 (accessed 8 March 2011).

[117]Ibid.

[118]Ibid.

[119]Audrey Kurth Cronin, *How Terrorism Ends: Understanding the Decline and Demise of Terrorist Campaigns* (Princeton, NJ: Princeton University Press, 2009), 206.

[120]Obama, Barack. *Remarks by the President on Osama Bin Laden,* whitehouse.gov, http://www.whitehouse.gov/the-press-office/2011/05/02/remarks-president-osama-bin-laden (accessed 12 June 2011).

[121]Cronin, 13.

[122]Jordan, et al., 42-3.

[123]Paul R. Pillar, *Terrorism and U.S. Foreign Policy* (Washington, DC: Brookings Institution Press, 2001), 8.

[124]Ibid., 29.

[125]Ibid., 73.

[126]Philip Seib, ‒The Al-Qaeda Media Machine," *Military Review* (May-June 2008), reprinted in *The Center for Army Lessons Learned Newsletter, No. 09-11* (Ft. Leavenworth, KS: Center for Army Lessons Learned, December 2008), 95.

[127]Bruce Hoffman, *Inside Terrorism*, rev. and expanded (New York, NY: Columbia University Press, 2006), 183-4.

[128]Ibid., 184.

[129]Paul Wilkinson, *Terrorism Versus Democracy* (London: Frank Cass Publishers, 2001), 201, 208.

[130]Ibid., 222.

[131]Ibid., 233.

[132]Daniel Whiteneck, ‒Deterring Terrorists: Thoughts on a Framework," *The Washington Quarterly* 28, no.3 (Summer 2005):187-199.

[133]Ibid.

[134]M. Elaine Bunn, ‒Can Deterrence Be Tailored?" (Strategic Forum, No. 225, Institute for National Strategic Studies, National Defense University, Washington, DC, January 2007), 1-7.

[135]Ibid.

[136]Ibid.

[137]European Union Naval Forces Somalia, ‒Mission," http://www. eunavfor.eu/about-us/mission/ (accessed 19 March 2011).

[138]Ibid.

[139]The International Institute for Strategic Studies, ‒Discussion Meeting - Karsten von Hoesslin," 23 February 2006, http://www.iiss.org/events-calendar/2006-events-

archive/february-2006/discussion-meeting---karsten-von-hoesslin/ (accessed 20 March 2011).

[140]European Union Naval Forces Somalia

[141]PressTV (Iran), ―Iran Anti-Piracy Force Guarded 400 Ships,‖ http://www.presstv.ir/detail/141471.html (accessed 20 March 2011).

[142]Trend (Azerbaijan), ―Iran Anti-Piracy Mission Independent,‖ http://en.trend.az/regions/iran/1827272.html (accessed 20 March 2011).

[143]Liu Dong, ―China Extends Anti-Piracy Effort Near Somalia,‖ *Global Times (China)*, http://en.huanqiu.com/china/diplomacy/2010-01/495999.html (accessed 20 March 2011).

[144]RusNavy.com, ―Russian Navy Plans to Dispatch 5 Anti-Piracy Task Units – RADM Shtukaturov,‖ http://rusnavy.com/news/navy/index.php?ELEMENT_ID=11742 (accessed 20 March 2011).

CHAPTER 5

CONCLUSIONS

This chapter reviews and summarizes the analysis from chapter 4, briefly lists and describes the constants and variables of containment strategies, suggests a bolstered emphasis on security cooperation and other phase zero education topics, and recommends expanded subject matter for further analysis.

Sufficient circumstantial evidence exists supporting the claim that certain components of containment can be effective against non-superpower targets, provided specific conditions are met. Like other phase zero conflict prevention activities however, causality cannot meet the ―beyond a reasonable doubt‖ burden of proof. Instead, a ―preponderance of the evidence‖ standard justifies continued efforts for constructing and executing contemporary containment strategies.

The research extracted and analyzed a list of containment constants and variables that have potential or actual applicability against modern non-super power targets, including non-state actors and terrorist organizations.

Containment Constants

First, to clarify the constants: its usage in the thesis means the factors were always observed, not that their values remained constant.

Patience

Since containment policies rarely address the root causes of the phenomenon being contained, ultimate victory takes years, if not decades to occur. Patience therefore is the most desirable condition, and it must be sufficiently in place at multiple levels. A containment policy without long-term buy-in from all branches of government is doomed to failure. Congress must be committed enough to authorize continued spending, whether during an economic boom period or during a recession. Presidents, whether Democrat or Republican, need to continue their predecessor's overall strategies, either fully or with tweaks and adjustments to fit their individual ideologies. Likewise, the voting public must support the policy, or be at least blissfully unaware of the policy enough not to protest it, lest their elected officials pull the plug on long-term support. Any containment policy that requires international assistance to be effective, which makes up the majority of such policies, additionally requires the same patience commitment levels as those in the U.S.

Eradication of terrorism, as a phenomenon, will not likely occur anytime soon. Weak actors, frequently unable or unwilling to shape their environment legitimately in accordance with their concepts and beliefs, will continue resorting to terrorist techniques. This long-term threat horizon reality then points to containment as an amenable option when considering various policies to fight terrorism.

Unlike many other areas where immediate results are expected, Americans have become conditioned and educated to the fact that the terrorism phenomenon is not something that can simply be targeted and destroyed quickly. Most understand that even the killing of Osama bin Laden, though psychologically very significant, will not signal the end of al Qaida, much less terrorism as a whole. This understanding is critical, because it implies the American public has the patience level required for a containment policy to have a reasonable chance of success. Despite complicated, expensive and globally interdependent containment strategy, Soviet threats of Communist expansion lasted decades. Short of declaration of war against the USSR, (almost unthinkable due to the counter opposing nuclear threats) versions of containment provided the most prudent option. The terrorism phenomenon likewise has long legs, with enduring, consistent, and cooperative containment strategy offering a viable course of action.

A generic containment policy focuses on, at least initially, deterring expansion of the target's capabilities and intentions. It maintains a firm belief that patience, consistency, unity of effort, and stubborn determination will eventually overcome those same attributes of its target. The U.S. and its Allies' enduring commitment to their Cold War Containment strategy did indeed outlast the determinations and capabilities of its primary target, the USSR. There is no reason to believe that a similar level of commitment against global terrorism will not enjoy similar results. Granted there are many more terrorism organizations professing almost as many different desired end states, but a consistent counter-terrorism strategy will eventually convince their leaders of the futility of their methods. Remember that deterrence derives from multiplying capability and credibility. A consistent containment policy goes a long way to establishing adequate levels of credibility.

Economic Benefit

A successful containment strategy promotes stability globally or regionally, depending on that strategy's focus. Stability preserves economies, again either globally or regionally depending on the stable area's scope. For instance, anytime instability threatens an oil-producing country or region, global markets react by driving petroleum products upward. An economic benefit always results from stability promotion, and therefore is always a constant of containment strategies.

Manageable Risk

Any successful containment strategy must include calculations accounting for, and managing the risks of the target entity's retaliation ability. These planning calculations ensure implementation of sufficient collateral-damage risk mitigation measures, as well as methods to inflict maximum damage to the target with minimal exposure to friendly forces.

Unity of Effort

Like the patience attribute, unity of effort requires cooperation for successful execution of any containment policy. The Department of Defense must be on the same page as the Departments of Homeland Security, Justice, Energy, State, and a host of other agencies. Conflicting ideas and philosophies, particularly if public, spell doom for long-term policies such as containment.

Allied Support

Any large-scale containment effort requires extraordinary cooperation from many nations. NATO became the ―Unity of Effort‖ face for the Cold War's containment of the USSR. The same remains true with the efforts against the Somali pirates and with the Global War on Terrorism. A single country or weak coalition aligned against either of these stands little chance of success. Demonstrated global resolve is a constant of any successful containment policy.

Relative Consistency

Historians debate whether détente's tendency to accommodate (or some may say appease) the Soviet Union actually prolonged the Cold War. Regardless, the overall U.S.

policies from Truman through Reagan remained consistent enough to eventually achieve its desired end state. ―Relative Consistency" then was an observed containment policy constant of the Cold War, and remains a constant for any modern application. For example, if a targeted terrorism organization believes the U.S. or any other enemy will cease operations against them after a set calendar date, it will simply wait until that time has elapsed before reasserting itself. If that organization remains convinced that the U.S. will continue its efforts at any time and at any place and without respite, their long-term calculus may eventually change.

Security Benefit

Without a perceived security benefit, no containment policy would ever be pursued for a long period. The Somalia case studies explain this, and are more fully described in the next section.

Containment Variables

Moral Values

This component can fit within the constants category as well as with the variables, because the U.S. consistently attempts to justify their actions, especially military operations, with appeals to morality. It nonetheless remains in the variable category due to its demonstrated inability to stand alone for a period long enough to create a successful containment policy.

The two Somalia case studies illustrate this point most effectively. While the initial international response to Somalia's situation in 1993 was inarguably morally correct, there was no perceived list of containment constants to bolster the case for a

141

long-term containment policy. Somalia offered no significant economic benefit to the world and posed little external security threat. Expending U.S. blood and treasure merely because it was the right thing to do was insufficient without additional return on investment.

The expansion of Somali pirate clan capabilities, and their increasing toll on maritime profitability however resulted in quite a different picture. In this case, all five primary containment constants existed in plentiful quantity. First, pirates posed an immediate security threat to the citizens of maritime countries. Next, they were having a direct impact on the prices consumers would have to absorb resulting from piracy and its associated costs. Countries shared adequate consistency of desired end states, even while differing on rules of engagement and pirate handling procedures. For the most part, they cooperated in anti-piracy efforts by sharing intelligence and other resources. Lastly, the biggest constant present among responding maritime governments however was their shared degree of patience. None of these countries committed military resources to large scale shore-based operations aimed at permanently eradicating Somali pirates, and instead consistently contented themselves with maintaining a network of ships, aircraft, and watch centers designed to contain, or manage piracy to reasonable levels. To be fair, the U.S., the European Union, and individual countries have designated considerable non-military resources toward solutions, but their relative unity of policy against in-country military action is remarkable.

Specific Target (State, Failed State, or Non-State Organization [e.g. Terrorists or Pirates])

This variable marks the most consistent difference between those who believe containment died along with the Soviet Union and those who believe it can be applied in other situations. This thesis admits that a containment policy targeting an established state has better odds at success than one aimed at either a failed state or non-state entity, mainly due to the former's heavier responsibilities to its broader populace. The idea that containment cannot be applied to anything other than a state is rejected however due to examples cited throughout this thesis, with specific emphasis on ongoing Somali piracy containment operations. The ―Specific Target" category therefore firmly belongs in the ―Variables" category. Targeting a state then is not essential for a containment policy to work, though it is undeniably helpful.

Application (Universal/Selective [Symmetrical/Asymmetrical])

The Cold War demonstrated that differing presidents favoring differing containment policies, whether symmetrically or asymmetrically oriented, remained consistent enough to eventually wear down the Soviet Union's ability to continue indefinitely. Debates continue regarding whether one policy style or another expedited or delayed the Kremlin's demise, but sufficient academic consensus concludes broad U.S. Containment policy was instrumental to its eventual defeat.

Current U.S. counter-terrorism policy targets organizations that have conducted operations outside the borders of their country of origin. Support may or may not be given to countries struggling with internal terrorist threats, but so far, a doctrine of asymmetrical terrorist containment seems to dominate U.S. foreign policy.

143

Likewise, asymmetrical thinking extends to anti-piracy policies. Large, well-funded task forces patrol waters along the Horn of Africa for Somali pirates. Much smaller, less consistent forces are available for lesser-known piracy hotspots, including areas within the Gulf of Guinea. A symmetrical anti-piracy policy would attempt to squash piracy wherever and whenever it appeared globally.

Threat (WMD, Conventional Terrorism, Economic Loss [e.g. Piracy])

The larger the perceived threat, the larger the potential exists for a country to develop a containment policy to defeat it. The Soviet Union's possession of a credible and capable nuclear force effectively deterred the U.S. or NATO from directly or deliberately starting a war. A containment policy was instead devised and relied on for the duration of the Cold War. Likewise, though on a much smaller scale, the painful memory of dead U.S. soldiers dragged through the streets of Mogadishu weighed heavily on the minds of politicians deciding how to address the current Somali piracy problem. Containment became the chosen course of action because it offered the safest option for its forces, while still promising manageable piracy levels and hope for its eventual demise.

Containment strategy, as a policy, offers the U.S. and the world a long-term management plan of unpleasant situations short of direct engagement or regime overthrow. It requires a great deal of collective patience, resources, and consistency. These strategies also rely heavily on deterrence principles, which are notoriously difficult to accurately measure effectiveness rates. These burdens must be fully understood and accepted prior to any attempt to devise new containment policies against either countries or phenomena.

Recommended Further Research

Analysis of additional case studies is recommended because of the added authority it would extend to this project. Containment of states and containment of phenomenon examples comprise two distinct categories for further research.

Recommended States for Further Research

Recommended states to study containment viability include the People's Republic of China, the Islamic Republic of Iran, and the Democratic People's Republic of Korea. China's inclusion is warranted because it represents the closest case study to the Cold War Soviet Union, yet has enough dissimilarity that a close analysis should shed light on whether a containment policy could work there. Iran, while not a super-power, may acquire nuclear weapons, and its frequent belligerent nature begs further analysis from a containment strategy standpoint. North Korea already possesses WMD, and frequently demonstrates aggressive actions and rhetoric. A containment viability study on North Korea is fascinating for many reasons, including the fact that China itself could serve as a quasi coalition partner with the U.S., even though China could be the target of a separate containment policy when divorced from the North Korea question.

Recommended Phenomenon Studies
for Further Research

Cyber security represents a current and growing threat to personal identities and finances, as well as national security. The nation (and world) is increasingly reliant on conducting day-to-day business through the internet. Credit, personal, and governmental information continues to be critically vulnerable to theft from hackers. Can an effective international cyber security containment policy be crafted? Upon first glance, cyber security meets the containment constants developed from this thesis analysis, and therefore deserves further study.

The global narcotics scourge presents another case for containment applicability. The —War on Drugs" moniker implies a conventional war that can be fought and won with a clear phase-line progression, yet reality seems to point to more of a management, or containment, of its effects. The counter-narcotics challenge also presents the additional twist of containing both the supply of drugs, as well as its demand.

Research DoD-Wide Training and Education Curricula

Current curriculum at the U.S. Army CGSC (ILE) program at Fort Leavenworth offers extremely limited topics about phase-zero conflict prevention activities. One needs look no further than the two available security cooperation courses offered during the elective period only. Less than 5 percent of the entire student population chose to take them, implying their perceived value and applicability was low. Additionally, war game scenarios conducted throughout ILE routinely glossed over any deterrence planning or execution, much less the creation and implementation of a containment strategy. They instead spend the vast majority of time, effort, and instruction on the lethal phases.

These author-observed conditions perceived the situation at a single DoD school, but anecdotal evidence derived from multiple discussions with CGSC faculty and fellow students point to probable wide-spread deficiencies in formalized phase-zero education.

146

Further research along these lines via DoD-wide surveys would confirm or deny these suspicions, and would lead to comprehensive solutions if required.

Suggested Immediate Fixes

The author, lacking results of DoD-wide educational surveys, can only recommend changes to curriculum observed first-hand at ILE, but the overall fix begins by requiring literal action on our own written operating concepts. Preventing war joins the traditional fighting and winning our nation's wars on an equal plane. This co-equality demands a fair share of training and educational resources and level of effort. Immediately incorporate security cooperation educational courses and other conflict prevention material into ILE's core curricula. The exercise scenarios need major overhauling, with multiple scripts and injects prewritten for inclusion depending on how, when, and where students decide to attempt deterrent measures, or even craft and test an encompassing containment plan.

Final Thoughts

Ultimately, the political weather vanes point toward future foreign policies more reliant on international cooperation rather than direct unilateral intervention. A broad comprehension of containment strategy historical application, along with prevalent war and foreign policy theory, offers politicians, planners, and practitioners the tools to contribute effectively to their nation's national security. It behooves the military professionals to understand more fully that ―full spectrum operations" involves preventive measures in addition to standard lethal options most frequently emphasized in the schoolhouse, field exercises, and actual operations.

So, is post-Cold War containment relevant to today's non-superpower security challenges? Case study paucity limited definitive answers to this original thesis question, but the analyzed results from the selected examples strongly hint in favor of continued relevance, given sufficient quantities and qualities of previously listed conditions. Despite the Cold War's thermometer-based adjective, its crucible experience yields applicable lessons for current leaders struggling to deal with threats unimaginable just a few decades earlier.

BIBLIOGRAPHY

Books

Allard, Kenneth. *Somalia Operations: Lessons Learned*. Washington, DC: National Defense University Press, 2004.

Bowden, Mark. *Black Hawk Down*. New York, NY: Signet Books, 1999.

Chesterman, Simon. *Just War or Just Peace?: Humanitarian Intervention and International Law*. New York, NY: Oxford University Press, 2001.

Cronin, Audrey Kurth. *How Terrorism Ends: Understanding the Decline and Demise of Terrorist Campaigns*. Princeton, NJ: Princeton University Press, 2009.

Dobbins, James, John G. McGinn, Keith Crane, Seth G. Jones, Rollie Lal, Andrew Rathmell, Rachel Swanger, and Anga Timilsina. *America's Role in Nation-Building: from Germany to Iraq*. Santa Monica, CA: RAND, 2003.

Dershowitz, Alan. *Preemption:A Knife that Cuts Both Ways*. New York, NY: W.W. Norton & Company Inc., 2006.

Freedman, Lawrence. *Deterrence*. Cambridge, UK: Polity Press, 2004.

Gaddis, John L. *The Cold War: A New History*. New York, NY: The Penguin Press, 2005.

————. *Strategies of Containment*. New York, NY: Oxford University Press, 1982.

Hoffman, Bruce. *Inside Terrorism, Revised and Expanded Edition*. New York, NY: Columbia University Press, 2006.

Jarecki, Eugene. *The American Way of War: Guided Missiles, Misguided Men, and a Republic in Peril*. New York, NY: Free Press, 2008.

Jordan, Amos A., William J. Taylor, Jr., and Michael J. Mazarr. *American National Security*, 5th ed. Baltimore, MD: The Johns Hopkins University Press, 1999.

Kahn, Herman. *On Thermonuclear War*. Princeton, NJ: Princeton University Press, 1960.

_____. *Thinking About the Unthinkable in the 1980s*. Indianapolis, IN: The Hudson Institute Inc., 1984.

Leedy, Paul D., and Jeanne E. Ormrod. *Practical Research Planning and Design*, 8th ed. Upper Saddle River, NJ: Pearson Education Inc., 2005.

Luttrell, Marcus. *Lone Survivor*. New York, NY: Little, Brown and Company, 2007.

Mearsheimer, John J. *The Tragedy of Great Power Politics*. New York, NY: W.W. Norton & Company Inc., 2001.

Merriam, Sharan B. *Qualitative Research and Case Study Applications in Education, Revised and Expanded from Case Study Research in Education*. San Francisco, CA: Jossey-Bass, 1998.

Netanyahu, Binyamin. *Fighting Terrorism: How Democracies Can Defeat the International Terrorist Network*. New York, NY: Farrar, Straus and Giroux, 2001.

Pillar, Paul R. *Terrorism and U.S. Foreign Policy*. Washington, DC: Brookings Institution Press, 2001.

Pirio, Gregory A. *The African Jihad: Bin Laden's Quest for the Horn of Africa*. Trenton, NJ: Red Sea Press, 2007.

Shapiro, Ian. *Containment: Rebuilding a Strategy Against Global Terror*. Princeton, NJ: University Press, 2007.

Smoke, Richard and Alexander L. George, *Deterrence in American Foreign Policy: Theory and Practice*. New York, NY: Columbia University Press, 1974.

Suskind, Ron. *The One Percent Doctrine*. New York, NY: Simon & Schuster Paperbacks, 2006.

Walzer, Michael. *Arguing about War*. New Haven, CT: Yale University Press, 2004.

Wilkinson, Paul. *Terrorism Versus Democracy*. London: Frank Cass Publishers, 2001.

Government Documents

BMP 3, *Best Management Practices to Deter Piracy off the Coast of Somalia and in the Arabian Sea Area, Version 3*. Edinburgh, Scotland, UK: Witherby Seamanship International Ltd., 3 June 2010.

Department of Defense. *Deterrence Operations Joint Operating Concept (DO JOC) Version 2.0*. Offutt Air Force Base, NE: U.S. Strategic Command, 2006.

———. Joint Publication 3-0, *Joint Operations*. Washington, DC: Joint Chiefs of Staff, 2008.

———. Joint Publication 5-0, *Joint Operation Planning*. Washington, DC: Joint Chiefs of Staff, 2010.

President of the United States. *The National Military Strategy of the United States of America, 2011 Redefining America's Military Leadership.* Washington, DC: Government Printing Office, 8 February 2011.

————. *The National Security Strategy of the United States of America, 2002.* Washington, DC: Government Printing Office, September 2002.

————. Office of the Special Assistant for National Security Affairs.Records, 1952-61, Memorandum for the National Security Council, *Project Solarium.* 22 July 1953. NSC Series, Subject Subseries Box No: 9, A67-50 & A67-64, Abilene, KS: Eisenhower Presidential Library,.

U.S. Army. Field Manual (FM) 1-02, *Operational Terms and Graphics.* Washington, DC: Department of the Army, 2010.

————. *Operating Concept 2016-2028 Version 2.0.* Washington, DC: Department of Defense, 2010.

U.S.Marine Corps, U.S. Navy and U.S. Coast Guard. *Naval Operations Concept 2010.* Washington, DC: Department of Defense, 2009.

Internet Sources

BBC News. "Rwanda: How the Genocide Happened." 18 December 2008. http://news.bbc.co.uk/2/hi/africa/1288230.stm (accessed 22 February 2011).

Brodie, Bernard. "The Anatomy of Deterrence." *World Politics* 11, no. 2 (January 1959). http://www.jstor.org/stable/2009527 (accessed 2 March 2011).

Combined Task Force (CTF) 151. "Mission Statement." January 2009. http://www. cusnc.navy.mil/cmf/151/index.html (accessed 21 February 2011).

Dong, Liu. "China Extends Anti-Piracy Effort Near Somalia." *Global Times (China).* http://en.huanqiu.com/china/diplomacy/2010-01/495999.html (accessed 20 March 2011).

European Union Naval Forces. "Operation Atalanta Media Information Guide." www.eunavfor.eu (accessed 19 March 2011).

European Union Naval Forces Somalia. "Mission." http://www.eunavfor.eu/about-us/mission/ (accessed 19 March 2011).

Freedman, Lawrence. "America Needs a Wider Coalition, However Difficult." *The Independent.* 29 March 2003. http://www.independent.co.uk/opinion/ commentators/lawrence-freedman-america-needs-a-wider-coalition-however-difficult-592696.html (accessed 15 January 2011).

Gaddis, John L. "Containment: Its Past and Future." *International Security* 5, no. 4 (Spring 1981). http://www.jstor.org/stable/2538714 (accessed 2 March 2011).

Gaddis, John L., and Paul Nitze. "NSC 68 and the Soviet Threat Reconsidered." *International Security* 4, no. 4 (Spring 1980). http://www.jstor.org/stable/ 2626672 (accessed 2 March 2011).

Glaser, Charles L. "Realists as Optimists: Cooperation as Self-Help." *International Security* 19, no. 3 (Winter 1994-1995). http://www.jstor.org/pss/2539079 (accessed 13 March 2010).

The International Institute for Strategic Studies. "Discussion Meeting - Karsten von Hoesslin." 23 February 2001. http://www.iiss.org/events-calendar/2006-events-archive/february-2006/discussion-meeting---karsten-von-hoesslin/ (accessed 20 March 2011).

Jantsch, John. "99% of Advertising Doesn't Sell a Thing." *Duct Tape Marketing*. 14 May 2006. http://www.ducttapemarketing.com/blog/2006/05/14/99-of-advertising-doesnt-sell-a-thing/ (accessed 25 October 2010).

Jervis, Robert. "The Impact of the Korean War on the Cold War." *The Journal of Conflict Resolution* 24, no. 4 (December 1980). http://www.jstor.org/stable/173775 (accessed 2 March 2011).

McLellan, David S. "Who Fathered Containment?: A Discussion." *International Studies Quarterly* 17, no. 2 (June 1973). http://www.jstor.org/stable/2600228 (accessed 2 March 2011).

McMillan, Pricilla Johnson. "Cold Warmonger." *New York Times*, 25 May 1997. http://query.nytimes.com/gst/fullpage.html?res=9800EEDA1438F936A15756C0 A961958260 (accessed 28 February 2011).

Morgenthau, Hans J. "The Four Paradoxes of Nuclear Strategy." *The American Political Science Review* 58, no. 1 (March 1964). http://www.jstor.org/stable/1952752 (accessed 20 March 2011).

Osman, Ali. "Op-Ed-Somalia: The Wrong Strategy." *Somalialand Press.com*. http://somalilandpress.com/op-ed-somalia-the-wrong-strategy-17410 (accessed 8 March 2011).

President of the United States. "Remarks by President on Osama Bin Laden." Whitehouse.gov. http://www.whitehouse.gov/the-press-office/2011/05/02/ remarks-president-osama-bin-laden (accessed 12 June 2011).

PressTV (Iran). "Iran Anti-Piracy Force Guarded 400 Ships." http://www.presstv.ir/ detail/141471.html (accessed 20 March 2011).

Rosen, Laura. ―Dual Containment and HRC's ‗Obliterate' Iran Remarks." *Mother Jones.com*. 8 May 2008. http://motherjones.com/mojo/2008/05/former-nsc-aide-clinton-dual-containment-and-hrcs-obliterate-iran-remarks (accessed 21 February 2011).

RusNavy.Com. ―Russian Navy Plans to Dispatch 5 Anti-Piracy Task Units–RADM Shtukaturov." http://rusnavy.com/news/navy/index.php?ELEMENT_ID=11742 (accessed 20 March 2011).

Stix, Nicholas. ―Containment Theory is Dead! Long Live Containment Theory!" ToogoodReports.com. 27 February 27. http://www.freerepublic.com/focus/f-news/853245/posts (accessed 2 March 2011).

Trend (Azerbaijan). ―Iran Anti-Piracy Mission Independent." http://en.trend.az/regions/iran/1827272.html (accessed 20 March 2011).

U.S. Department of State. ―Policy Statement of U.S.-Iranian Relations." http://www.state.gov/r/pa/ei/bgn/5314.htm (accessed 21 February 2011).

U.S. Forces Korea. ―Commander's Vision & Priorities." http://www.usfk.mil/usfk/content.usfk.vision.28 (accessed 21 February 2011).

United Nations Security Council. ―Preamble." UNSCR 733, *United Nations Security Council Resolution 733*. 1992. http://daccess-dds--ny.un.org/doc/resolution/gen/nr0/010/92/img/nr001092.pdf (accessed 13 June 2011).

———. UNSCR 837, *United Nations Security Council Resolution 837*. 1993. http://daccess-dds-ny.un.org/doc/undoc/gen/n93/332/32/img/n9333232.pdf (accessed 13 June 2011).

———. UNSCR 1973, *United Nations Security Council Resolution 1973*. 2011. http://daccess-dds-ny.un.org/doc/undoc/gen/n11/268/39/pdf/n1126839.pdf (accessed 13 June 2011).

Other Sources

Bunn, M. Elaine. ―Can Deterrence Be Tailored?" Strategic Forum, No. 225, Institute for National Strategic Studies, National Defense University, January 2007.

Davis, Robert T. II. ―The US Army and the Media in the 20th Century." Occasional Paper 31. Fort Leavenworth, KS: Combat Studies Institute Press, July 2009.

Gray, Colin S. ―The Implications of Preemptive and Preventive War Doctrines: A Reconsideration." Monograph, Strategic Studies Institute, Carlisle Barracks, PA, 2007.

McNeil, Samuel L. ─Achieving a Credible Nuclear Deterrent." *Air & Space Power Journal* (Fall 2010): 21-8.

Pickett, W. B., ed. ─George F. Kennan and the Origins of Eisenhower's New Look: An Oral History of Project Solarium." Monograph Series Number 1, Princeton Institute for International and Regional Studies, Princeton University, 2004.

Seib, Philip. The Al-Qaeda Media Machine." *Military Review* (May-June 2008), reprinted in *The Center for Army Lessons Learned Newsletter, No. 09-11.* December 2008.

Whiteneck, Daniel. ─Deterring Terrorists: Thoughts on a Framework." *The Washington Quarterly* 28, no. 3 (Summer 2005).

www.ingramcontent.com/pod-product-compliance
Lightning Source LLC
Chambersburg PA
CBHW080251290526
45790CB00005B/1769